Kitchen
Basics

Diana Peacock

—

Baking Bread

Easy techniques for making all types
of bread at home

Kitchen
Newbie

A Kitchen Newbie Book

For my mum, Millicent Sutton.
She taught me what great happiness and
contentment can be found in baking.

A Kitchen Newbie Book

First published in Great Britain in 2017 by Kitchen Newbie
Copyright © Diana Peacock 2017

Diana Peacock asserts her moral right under the Copyright, Designs and Patents Act, 1988 to
be identified as the author of this work.

All rights reserved. No part of this book may be reproduced, stored in a retrieval system,
or transmitted in any form or by any means, electronic, electrostatic, magnetic tape,
mechanical, photocopying, recording, or otherwise without permission in writing from the
author.

Important note:
It is particularly important to keep all utensils, surfaces and equipment clean and sterilised.
In no circumstances can the publisher or author accept any legal responsibility or liability
for any loss or damage (including personal injury) arising from any error or omission from
the information contained in this book, or from the reader failing properly and accurately to
follow any instructions contained within this book.

Illustrations by Rebecca Wright
Printed and bound by CreateSpace

www.kitchennewbie.com

Contents

Introduction	07
1 A short(crust) history	**09**
2 Ingredients & utensils	**15**
Types of flour	15
Raising agents	18
Salt	20
Liquid	21
Fat	21
Extras	22
Utensils	25
3 Techniques	**29**
Breadmaking stages	29
Bread shapes	35
4 Family bread recipes	**39**
5 Breads from around the world	**59**
6 Sweetened breads	**83**
7 Celebration breads	**103**
8 Gluten-free breads	**113**
9 Cooking with bread	**117**
10 When things go wrong	**141**
Index	149

Introduction

The Staff of Life

Throughout history bread, or derivations of bread, have comforted and sustained us. It is an essential weekly purchase and a 'must have' in all but a few households. Its versatility made it a snack food eaten 'on the hoof' long before the idea of fast food became a feature of the high street. We feed it to our children when they are beginning to feed themselves and it is often the main item in their lunch boxes when they go to school.

A slice of toasted bread is the only thing I could ever face early in the morning before going to work and it remains a favourite breakfast and supper food in our house. Whilst the smell of freshly baked bread has a strong, emotive pull, a lettuce sandwich eaten a few hours before retiring to bed is also an old remedy for aiding sleep.

The great thing about bread is that one never tires of eating it as it comes in so many different forms, flavours and textures. It is a useful ingredient in many recipes from sandwiches to breadcrumbs, as a binding agent in sausages and puddings and is also used to coat many foods before frying. The versatility of bread is easily overlooked as it is often underused in other recipes. It is my hope in writing this book that more people will be encouraged to go back to making their own bread in as natural a way as possible.

It is clear after talking to many different kinds of people from school children and teachers to friends of all ages, that most of us love the idea of homemade bread and everyone is impressed that it can be done so easily.

The purpose of this book is not to explain how to use bread-making machines as their use is often self-explanatory and, though they are widely used, I hope this book will inspire the reader to make bread using their own hands. Having said this, I do feel for those who find kneading dough difficult and a mixer using dough hooks can be very useful, and give excellent results too. So do enjoy reading this and enter into a new area of bread eating and bread making.

Diana Peacock

Chapter One

A Short(crust) History

Baking with grain-based foodstuffs can be traced back to the Middle East in approximately 17,000 BC and archeological work has found evidence of the organised arable farming of grain in 10,000 BC.

Ancient Egyptian artefacts prove that growing wheat for bread was widespread and there is artwork and hieroglyphic evidence of the use of grain in everyday food production. Nearer to home, in Britain, we were making bread in the Stone Age using an ancient form of wheat called Emmer which is similar to Durum wheat that is used in the making of pasta.

Until the Roman invasion all dough was cooked on an open fire in Britain. What the Romans 'did for us' was to introduce enclosed ovens similar to the large pizza ovens we use today. Wheat was still the most popular grain used in bread making, however, when the Romans departed, the use of wheat declined and rye became more popular due to its higher yield.

In the Middle Ages bread was a status symbol, the rich eating 'Manchets' which were whiter, wheaten loaves whilst the poor ate a darker, coarser bread called 'Maslin' which was made from rye but also often contained weed seeds, ground legumes and sometimes even acorns.

So important was bread as a source of food that through periods of harsh weather when crops of cereal failed, severe famines occurred causing widespread revolt. As a result, the ruling classes attempted to prevent the prices of grain and bread from rising to high.

In the nineteenth century the price of grain still had a great impact on society. The government stated that England was not allowed to import 'corn' (a word used to cover all grains) until its price rose above a certain level. This was to protect the English landowners who grew grain from losing out to cheaper products from overseas.

The workers, unable to feed their families because of the cost of bread, protested and rose up, resulting in the powerful and influential anti-Corn Law movement, After much unrest the unpopular Corn Laws were removed and landowners had to compete with cheap foreign imports of grain, therefore having to grow their wheat more efficiently.

The significance of bread as a food staple carried on throughout the twentieth century when the allocation of bread to the troops in two world wars became a necessity and feeding people at home was more difficult. Governments have even used bread as a means of providing the people with a balanced diet by adding certain vitamin supplements to mass produced loaves. In fact, no other single foodstuff has carried so much historical importance as our beloved loaf.

These days bread is still a staple food in our diet and there is a great variety of flour and ready made bread available to us in the shops. It is a valuable source of carbohydrates, many necessary vitamins and minerals and, to a lesser degree, protein. Bread makes a quick meal in our very busy lives and people with a gluten free diet can still enjoy eating a loaf made with gluten-free flour. This a blend of grains using rice, tapioca, potato and maize flours.

Although most people in the UK buy their bread from large supermarkets, small artisan bakers' shops as seen throughout France are making a comeback here, with big chain bakers remaining commercially successful by selling pies and many other traditional items baked 'in-store'. I still get a thrill from seeing a local baker with a shop full of their own bread and each one often having a signature loaf baked to a secret recipe known only to their family.

We also have the added luxury of enjoying bread products from other countries; from croissants and brioches to bagels and rye cobs. There are many popular products from around the globe and I have included some of these recipes in this book. We even have local bread recipes from various regions in the British Isles, many with their own histories and stories attached and some with recipes zealously protected by the local people as an integral part of their own regional heritage.

Simply the best

I will not make up a wonderful, romantic story about how I always ate homemade bread as a child. This was certainly not the case, but we did always eat bread made in the small local bakery on our high street and it was very good. Making bread wasn't something my Mum ever did when I was young. She was a wonderful cook and she became famous for the pies she made with her hand made pastry, but as far as bread making is concerned I introduced my Mum to the glories of baking this staple.

When I was in high school, the highlight of my week was Thursday afternoon. We had a triple lesson of what was then called 'Domestic Science' taught by a lovely lady called Miss Braddock. She had her very grey hair tied back in a neat bun and the gentlest of dispositions which enabled her to scold with the merest whisper. I was entranced by her enthusiasm for cooking everything from jam tarts to shepherd's pie but one week, at the end of a lesson, Miss Braddock told us what we would be making in the next lesson. It was going to be bread or, as Miss B. said, 'You will be experiencing how to make your very own loaf of bread'.

Whilst it sounded exciting, little did I know what a great pleasure it was and still is. I always get a tingle of pleasure seeing my new bread emerge from the oven and even now I still ask if it's okay - not so much because I'm worried about it, but because I love hearing how much the family likes it.

I still buy bread from various bakers and sometimes from supermarkets. There are some excellent branded loaves, usually the seeded or multi-grain breads and my family love what is known as 'tiger bread', which can be purchased from most supermarkets. It is not always convenient to make your own and I wholeheartedly believe that it should never be seen as a chore but rather as a pleasure. Eating other people's bread has the added advantage of giving you further ideas for new flavours or shapes of loaves and also helps confirm just how easily this remarkable product can be made at home.

Learning about bread

I am constantly learning about varieties of bread, the vast array of grains that can be used, the seemingly endless ways of cooking the dough and how you can use the finished product in other dishes. The main reason for making your own bread is health and the fact that you will know exactly what has gone into it. Knowledge of ingredients has become ever more important in recent years, especially when you consider the additives that can be used legally in foodstuffs sold in shops.

Reading down the list of ingredients used in a well known brand of ordinary sliced white loaf there were four E numbers listed. Two were harmless emulsifiers and a preserver which inhibits mould growth, but one caused alarm. E920, L-Cysteine, is a flour 'improver' that creates a more stretchy dough, making bread lighter and more full of holes. It sells you air rather than bread so, in other words, it means the bread is made cheaper to make by using this ingredient.

You can alter the amount of salt in homemade bread to suit your personal taste and dietary requirements. Knowing the salt content in shop bought bread is useful and it is usually printed on the label, although some shop bought brand loaves don't do this as they can conceal any ingredient which may be a constituent part of another ingredient.

A basic recipe for a loaf of plain, home-baked bread only requires four ingredients, so seeing a chart listing ten or twelve ingredients on a loaf of bread seems a little ridiculous but this is why a mass-produced loaf tastes so different from a homemade one.

Baking bread is good for you

Baking your own bread is an excellent stress reliever and very good for you. Pummelling and pulling the dough takes quite a substantial amount of energy and, if you feel so inclined, you can imagine the dough is whoever has last angered you (although of course I have never done this!).

Now regarded as a rural classic, William Cobbett wrote in *Cottage Economy* (1823) 'Let a woman bake a bushel once a week and she will do very well without phials and gallipots.' Phials and gallipots were medicines and potions to cure illnesses. I don't know how true this idea for keeping one healthy is, woman or man, but I do know the more often I bake my own bread the better I feel and it certainly beats the gym for strengthening your hands and arm muscles. It also gives you a feeling of contentment knowing the bread is made by your own hand and that it is something others will enjoy.

Finally, baking bread at home has never been easier than it is today. The yeast ingredients are particularly easy to use (this is explained in depth in Chapter Three) and there is ever more variety to choose from. There is also a wider choice of flours available to us, from strong white to granary and all the variations in between and the quality is more consistent than it was a generation ago. There is quite a horrific story in Mancunian folklore about a local miller adding ground human bones to his flour as he worked close to the Manchester plague pit, an un-flagged grave containing many bodies. He was supposedly seen digging up skeletons at night and taking them back to his mill. This may just be a story to entertain or scare people, but the addition of chalk to flour was indeed proven true. This was done to whiten the flour and keep the cost down. Quality control these days would, of course, never allow additions such as this.

Most supermarkets stock various flours and makes and a few actually have their own brand of bread flour in white, brown and wholemeal ranges. Utensils have also never been better. Whereas you may use simple multi-purpose baking tins and sheets, there are also some very high-tech ones which make the job both easier and more successful. (Read more about this in Chapter Two)

Baking your own bread is a sensual experience. You rely on your sense of touch when making the dough and can feel it change as you mix and knead it. Whilst the bread is cooking you can also smell the aroma, which many people describe as one of their all time favourites and of course you will see and taste the finished product. So that's already four senses engaged in the process!

As this all this wasn't enough to tempt you to have a go at home bread making, one of the main reasons for doing it for me is the feeling of accomplishment and pride as you lift the bread out of the oven. The added bonus, though, is hearing the continuous compliments your family and friends bestow on you every time they taste it. A close friend came to visit just after I had finished baking a batch of loaves. He was amazed and said it was very impressive seeing all the bread piled up on the cooling tray.

Bread making doesn't have to be complicated. As a starting point, a basic white loaf can give you the same feeling of contentment as making one of the most advanced types of bread.

Chapter Two
────────

Ingredients & Utensils

This can be both the easiest and yet the most complicated part of making your own bread as the simplest recipe contains only four ingredients; flour, yeast, salt and water. To vary your bread making and eating experience, however, there are many different flours and other ingredients you may add to the mixture.

Flour

If we are going to look at the various ingredients used in bread making, the best place to begin is with flour in its many forms. Shops now sell a wide range of bagged flours for making bread. There are various mixes of grains and textures of wheat flours which provide a wide variety for easy bread making. However, they are quite expensive and can make home baking cost more than shop bought bread but purchasing the basic strong white, brown and wholemeal flours plus any other grains separately can bring the cost down considerably.

Wheat Flour

The wheat grain is composed of three parts: bran, germ and the endosperm. The object of milling grains is to separate the endosperm from the bran and the germ. This produces the popular white flour. The different types of flour contain the other two components in varying degrees. To make bread it is best to use a strong flour as this produces the best overall loaf. Its high gluten content makes the dough elastic and gives the finished loaf its substance, volume and texture. All wheat flours suitable for making bread will say 'strong plain flour' on the packet. Wheat flour is what most commercially baked bread is made from and other grain based flours may be added to it to vary the texture and flavour. I have used ordinary plain flour to bake bread if I ever run out out of strong, but I don't leave this bread to prove for as long as the diminished gluten content will affect the finished result - it could flop over.

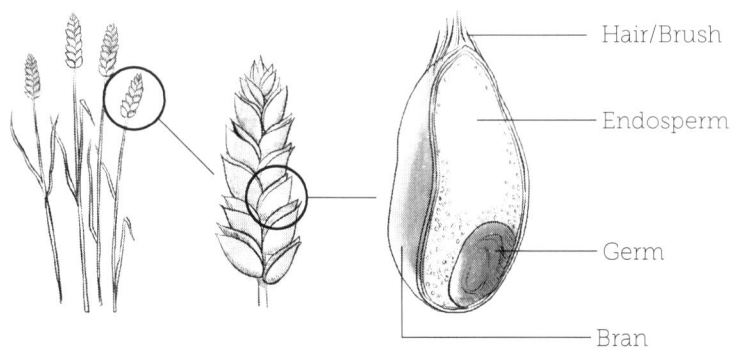

White
This is probably the most popular flour to begin with, as it is easiest to handle.

Wholemeal
This contains the whole grain, including the bran.

Wheatmeal
This is similar to wholemeal but with some of the coarser bran removed.

Brown
Contains 10-15% less bran than wholemeal.

Soft Grain
Uses white flour with added kibbled wheat or rye grains.

Country Malted
Has malted wheat flakes added to give a nutty flavour and an interesting texture.

Granary

With malted whole grains added to wholemeal

Rye Flour

This can be made into bread but it has a low gluten content so it is often mixed with wheat flour. The more rye flour used, the denser and more crumbly the texture of the finished bread. Rye is the main ingredient in the dark German pumpernickel bread.

Buckwheat

This flour is unsuitable for making bread. It isn't actually wheat and has no gluten in the flour. It makes very good pancakes, Russian blinis and French galettes.

Oatmeal

This is a wonderful ingredient in bread as it adds flavour, texture and nutritional value. However, is cannot be used as the only grain to make bread due to the lack of gluten.

Cornmeal or Maize

This can be ground into flour to make bread. A typical recipe would still use a half quantity of wheat flour. Cornbread is very popular in the United States as are corn fritters. Cornmeal or Polenta may be added to bread recipes to give texture to the finished loaf.

Cornflour

This is used to lighten shortbread and cakes and to thicken sauces.

Soya Flour

This cannot be used on its own to make bread as it is gluten free, but due to its high protein content (almost twice as much as wheat flour) makes a good addition to the ingredients list. A recipe shouldn't, however, contain more than 10-20% soya flour as the final result would become very heavy and inedible.

Gram Flour

This flour is made from ground chickpeas and is gluten free. It is used in Asian cookery to make pakoras and bhajis. In Italy gram flour is used to make crisp pizza like pancakes called Farinata. The flour is mixed with water and olive oil, then cooked on a griddle. The French call the flour Socca and it is used in the Nice region to make a thick porridge which, when cold may be sliced, fried and served with sugar.

Rice Flour
This is often used to make pastries in Asian cookery but is not generally used in bread making.

Potato Flour
This is almost pure starch and is used as a thickening agent in dishes but potatoes can make delicious breads and flat breads (see recipe section).

Raising Agents

Flour is the main ingredient in any bread recipe, but most doughs require a raising agent to produce the correct texture and popular finished product.

The most widely used of these is yeast, but baking soda or baking powder is also used to make a loaf. Buttermilk is often used in conjunction with baking soda as its acidity helps to boost the rising of the dough in both soda breads and scones.

Yeast
Yeast can be bought in various forms, some easier to use than others, but most giving the same overall product. Yeast for baking bread is either fresh or dried.

Yeast is alive when used in baking and needs certain conditions to fulfil its job properly. The job of the yeast is to cause the dough to rise which it does because of the gas produced by the yeast which is released in certain conditions. It requires warmth, food and liquid. The liquid is either milk, water or a combination of both. The liquid is heated but not hot or boiling as this would kill the yeast and therefore stop it working in the dough. A small amount of sugar is mixed with the yeast to provide the food. When these conditions prevail the yeast can then get to work.

The gas produced that causes the dough to rise is carbon dioxide which comes from a breakdown of sugar to release energy. The energy produced makes more yeast in the dough as it reproduces. The carbon dioxide is simply

Ingredients & Utensils

a waste product which the yeast then ejects, allowing the bread to rise.

Fresh Yeast

This is sold in a compressed block and is a fawn/beige colour. It is sold by weight and a piece is cut for use from the main block. It should look moist with a fresh aroma. If the yeast looks dry or darker in colour in places and smells acidic it should not be used as it may be contaminated. If required fresh yeast may be stored in the fridge for several days and can be frozen successfully. If it is frozen it must be thoroughly thawed at room temperature before it is used in baking. It must be combined with a little warm water and a pinch of sugar and left in a warm place until the mixture is frothy. This shows that the yeast is working and can be used in recipes. Dried yeast comes in three basic forms:

Standard Dried Yeast

This is granulated and needs to be reconstituted before use. Mixing it with warm water and a little sugar does this. The manufacturer will recommend quantities. This can then be used as fresh yeast.

Easy-blend Dried Yeast

This is fine granules of yeast that may be added straight to the dry ingredients in the bread recipe. The liquid required is then added to both the yeast and the other dry ingredients together.

Fast-action Easy-blend Dried Yeast

This is also in the form of fine granules and is added to the dry ingredients at the beginning of the recipe. The reason it is called fast-action is that it speeds up the rising of the dough so only one period of proving is necessary before cooking. The ingredient added to the yeast which enables this speedier action is ascorbic acid or vitamin C.

The latter is the most widely available of yeast types and I have found it the easiest to use for everyday bread making. But using the Easy-blend dried yeast is also very easy and can give a better result as the dough requires two proving times, making it a lighter finished product. I very rarely use fresh yeast as it is so difficult to obtain, but it is good to have a go at baking your bread with it. I enjoy watching how the yeast works in the warm liquid as it bubbles and shows that it is ready to be added to the flour. On the whole, though, fast-action yeast has proved how easy it is to make your own bread and is the most popular form of yeast in use today.

Soda

Bread can be made without using yeast as its raising agent. For instance bicarbonate of soda is a leavening agent which is used in Soda bread. Soda bread originates from Ireland and was traditionally cooked in a covered pot over an open fire. The soda is activated by the addition of an acidic liquid such as buttermilk. It starts to produce carbon dioxide in the mixture, causing the dough to rise as soon as the liquid is added to the flour and soda. It is therefore a fast raising agent. Proving isn't necessary as it rises as it cooks rather like a cake would. It is a very quick way to make a loaf of bread, but it doesn't keep fresh for as long as yeast based mixtures. It really is better eaten whilst still warm or on the same day as baking.

Working without raising agents

Not all bread recipes call for the mixture to use a raising agent. There are many recipes for flat breads from throughout the world included in the recipe section.

Salt

We have covered two of the main ingredients in bread making; the flour and the raising agent. The next important addition is salt. Without this the bread would taste very odd.

When I was young my Mum regularly bought her bread from our local baker at the bottom of our road. The bread was baked in the back of the shop by a couple called George and Katie and, after baking the bread, they would then serve the customers at opening time. Often I would go with my Mum as the shop opened at about 7:45 am. Then we would go home and have fresh bread for breakfast before I went to school. Many families in the surrounding area would do this, so much so that most of the available bread was sold out by 8:30 am. One morning we got home and sat down to our meal of warm bread and butter. It was revolting and Mum ran back to the shop together with many other people following. George and Katie had forgotten to add the salt to their dough, so a whole batch of bread was wasted. At that time any waste food was sent to the local pig farmer. I remember being late for school alongside many others because of this catastrophe. After that the locals never let them forget the salt again, always asking, 'Is there salt in this lot?'

Salt is always added to the flour and mixed in before the yeast is incorporated as salt slows down the reaction of the yeast and stops it working as efficiently. But it is diluted enough when added to the flour for this not to be a problem in making bread.

Liquid

The liquid used to make bread may be water, milk or a combination of both. Some dessert bread recipes call for other liquids like fruit juices. This is always warm in yeast cookery as it requires heat to begin doing its job. It must not, however, be too hot as this would kill the yeast. The ideal temperature is warm to the touch, so always dip in a finger to test it before adding it to the rest of the ingredients.

Fat

If made with these four ingredients your bread will taste good and keep for a day or so, but no longer. For bread to remain fresh for longer one needs to add some fat or oil to the mixture. This can be butter, lard or a butter-style spread which is rubbed into the flour before adding the yeast. However, I tend to use oil as it is simply added to the dough with the liquid. Butter may be melted gently over a very low heat to be added in a similar way to oil. This is often called for in sweetened doughs as it gives a rich, creamy flavour and a softer finished product.

Any good quality oil will do, the choice depends entirely on your own taste. I tend to use either rapeseed, sunflower or olive oil. Extra virgin oil gives a particularly good flavour to bread and is often used to make Italian Focaccia.

Other highly flavoured oils like sesame or walnut should be added carefully and should be used in conjunction with a flavourless oil or the taste would be too overpowering and spoil the bread.

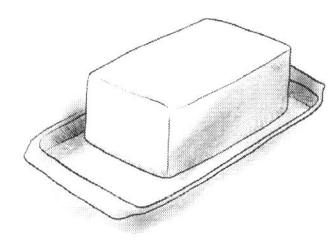

Optional Extras

Other additions to bread are the many seeds, herbs, nuts and grains that change the flavour and texture of the bread. They may be added to white, brown or wholemeal flours during the preparation of the dough and make a tasty alternative to a plain loaf.

Seeds

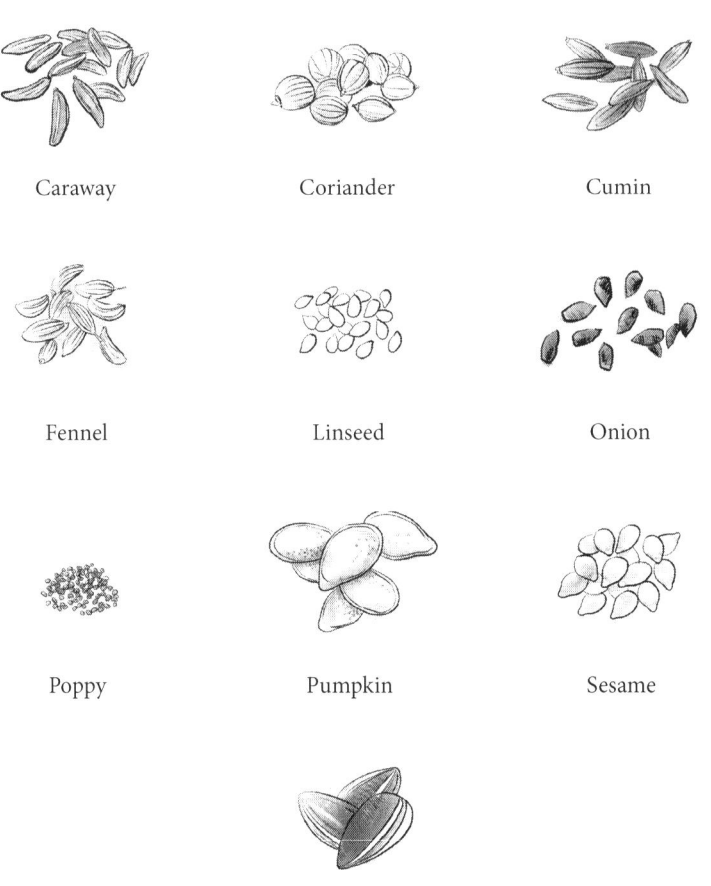

Caraway	Coriander	Cumin
Fennel	Linseed	Onion
Poppy	Pumpkin	Sesame
	Sunflower	

Ingredients & Utensils

Herbs

Chives

Dill

Marjoram

Parsley

Rosemary

Sage

Tarragon

Thyme

Nuts

Almond

Cashew

Hazelnut

Peanut

Pecan

Walnut

Grains

Barley

Oats

Toasted Wheat Rye

In sweetened dough dried fruits such as raisins, sultanas, candied peels, currants, cranberries, apples, prunes, pineapple, mangoes, cherries, pears, figs and dates are often added.

In savoury breads you can add ingredients such as sun-dried tomatoes, olives, peppers, caramelised onions and cheese.

In dessert breads an egg is often used to enrich the dough. This gives the finished bread a creamy taste and the soft texture most associated with sweetened breads.

Vitamin C

Vitamin C is regularly added to the yeast to improve its efficiency and the speed at which it begins to work within the dough. It also strengthens the gluten in the wheat so you get a better end product that is lighter and more uniformly risen. This is why you will find the word 'IMPROVER' in the list of ingredients on a commercially produced loaf. It is simply vitamin C. In the past, rose-hip syrup was added to the yeast as the combined sugar and vitamin C content helped kick-start the yeast into action.

Acids

In soda bread cookery the softness and light texture is achieved by adding an acidic ingredient to the flour and soda mixture. This is usually in the form of the liquid ingredient in the recipe, the milk. Buttermilk is naturally acidic and is often used in making a soda loaf, but adding a tablespoon of lemon juice to ordinary milk works equally well. If you find yourself with some milk that has just turned sour, don't waste it. Use at least some of it in baking soda bread. Souring milk is also acidic and makes excellent bread and scones, but do make sure it isn't too far gone or too solid.

This book has many different recipes for you to try. The quantities and

Ingredients & Utensils   25

variety of ingredients will enable to experiment and find your own personal favourites. I have no doubt forgotten some and you will discover more. Bread recipes can easily be changed or adapted very successfully.

Utensils

The next part of this chapter looks at the basic utensils you will need to make your bread. Some are for more specific baking needs so there is no need to rush out and buy everything mentioned in the following pages.

Oven
Bread needs to be baked at high temperature to kill the yeast, so an oven that reaches at least 225ºC/gas mark 8 is a must. Bread bakes equally well in all types of ovens and we have just acquired a small brick and clay oven in our garden which makes great bread and has that authentic edge to it.

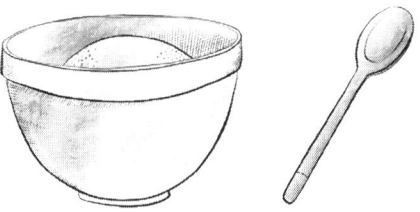

Mixing the dough
A large mixing bowl is needed even if you only make a small quantity of dough, as it is much easier to work with and keeps the heat of the mixture fairly constant, helping with the proving of the dough. I use a plastic bowl to make my bread as I find ceramic ones too heavy for me to carry around the kitchen when full of dough, but they are better at insulating the mixture than a plastic or metal bowl. Metal bowls are the least effective at keeping the dough warm so don't use them for bread making.

I prefer to mix the dry and liquid ingredients together with a large wooden spoon before getting my hands in. You can also use a metal spoon but I find a wooden one easier and quicker to use.

Baking pans and trays

Depending on the shape of the bread you want to make you will need a good quality baking tray or several if you wish to make small rolls. Non-stick bakeware isn't necessary. I use one of each and both work equally well so long as they are lightly oiled before the dough is placed on them. Baking trays are needed to make small or large sized cobs and loaves, but to make a traditional shaped loaf you will need a loaf tin. These can be made of steel with or without a non-stick coating but I have found an invaluable one made of silicone. This never needs oiling and is totally non-stick but because it is pliable and wobbly, I find it easier to handle if you place the container on a baking sheet before it goes in the oven rather than straight onto the oven rack. If you want perfectly formed small rolls this can be done by using a muffin tin. The shapes make perfect little cobs which are very cute and guaranteed to impress your dinner guests.

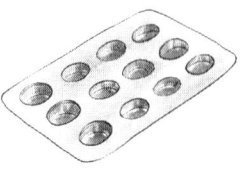

Loaf tins

Muffin tin

Cooling racks

Cooling racks are a must as the bread needs the air to circulate around it or the crust will lose its crispness and become soggy. This is due to the moisture exuding from the bread while it is still hot. Once it is cool this stops and the bread can then be kept in a covered container like any other bread.

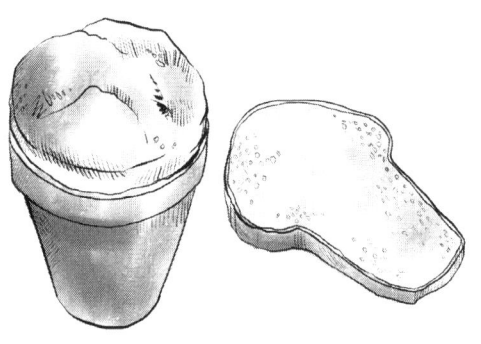

Terracotta

Terracotta makes an excellent container for cooking bread and the various size plant pots available are often used to make unusual shaped loaves. They need oiling well as the dough really sticks to the sides which can spoil the shape of the finished product. Using baking paper to line your pots stops the dreaded sticking to the sides of the pot. I have actually bought some pots of varying sizes for this job as the loaf slices in an interesting shape and looks good on the plate. Earthenware pots and dishes are very versatile as they can be used for a wide variety of recipes, not just for bread making.

Flat bread pans

To make tortilla and chapati style bread you will need a heavy based, good quality, flat-bottomed frying pan or griddle. The pan needs to get very hot and remain so till all the pieces of bread are cooked, so the best quality pan you can afford will stand you in good stead for all sorts of recipes.

Chapter Three

Techniques

Bread making, just like any other form of cookery, is a combination of both science and art. The science is how the ingredients work together during preparation and cooking. The art is understanding the ingredients, judging when you have to tweak a recipe and how the finished product is viewed. Knowing the techniques involved in making bread and why they are used helps us to understand the way bread is successfully made.

The ingredient that fascinates and sometimes alarms most people the most is the yeast. This is probably because it needs precise conditions to do its job successfully. A little knowledge about yeast should help to subdue any worries about using it.

As I have already explained yeast requires warmth, food and moisture to reproduce. A warm kitchen is therefore required when baking bread and all the dry ingredients must be at room temperature. The food for yeast is always sugar in some form or another and the liquid added to the dough provides the moisture. These three simple conditions allow the yeast to thrive and in doing so will work the miracle of producing a soft well risen loaf of bread. The yeast will simply produce carbon dioxide as it respires, so the dough rises and produces the effect we are expecting.

Steps to making a successful loaf

It is a good idea to begin by cleaning the surface you will be using to make your bread. I often use basic table salt to sterilise the surface; a liberal sprinkling on the work top can then be scrubbed in by hand, and then wiped away with water and a clean cloth. The abrasive nature of the salt crystals will lift up any dirt and kill bacteria. If you would prefer to use an antibacterial spray, make sure it is rinsed off and dried before you put your dough onto the surface, to avoid contaminating the mixture with chemicals.

As yeast needs warmth to activate, it is also a good idea to warm your bowl. I usually boil the kettle, pour in the hot water and then pour it away carefully. Dry the bowl with a towel and the bowl will be nicely warm by the time you come to use it.

1. Preparing the yeast

If you are using fresh or ordinary dried yeast then begin by making a ferment mixture which will consist of the yeast, the warm liquid from the recipe and a teaspoon of sugar. Stir this well and leave it in a warm place for 20-30 minutes until it is frothy.

2. Making the dough

The basic method for bread making is very simple. Sift the flour and salt together into a warm mixing bowl and rub in the fat if using it in the recipe. Add the ferment mixture and combine well with a wooden spoon.

3. Kneading

The next step is to knead the dough. This is an important stage in bread making as it determines the outcome of the finished loaf. Some people like a firm, dense texture to their bread and so do very little kneading of the dough. Most people, on the other hand, prefer a softer, lighter dough, therefore a good kneading is essential.

Kneading is mostly done by hand although it can be done with a mixer and dough hooks. These are very useful for anyone with arthritis in their hands or any other debilitating problem. The dough does require the kneading process as this action develops the gluten in the flour and produces soft, springy bread that will hold its shape.

The action of kneading is simple enough and you will get used to it the more you do it. I prefer to do it in the mixing bowl as it keeps the dough warm and helps with the shape, but most people knead the dough on a lightly floured

Techniques

surface. Try both ways and see which is easier for you.

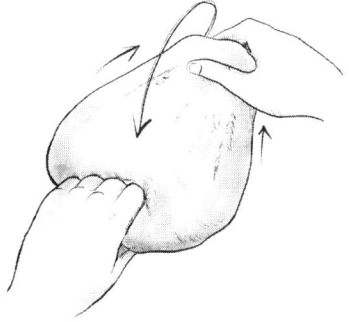 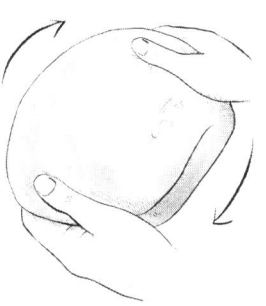

Hold the dough with one hand and pull at it with the other. Fold back over itself.

Turn the dough through 90° and repeat the process of kneading.

Hold the dough steady with one hand and pull at it with the other. Pull at the edge and stretch it away from you, then fold it back over the bulk of the dough. Turn through 90° and repeat this action constantly for 10 minutes. Any less than this and the bread won't be as soft and light. Correctly kneaded, the dough has a smooth appearance. It should look firm and have an elastic texture. If you gently prod it with your finger to form a 'dimple' it should recover quickly.

Wholemeal or granary flour may require a longer kneading time. It is very difficult to over knead by hand, but it may happen if you use a machine and this can cause a problem with the bread holding its shape. Over kneading can loosen the elasticity and spoil the finished product. So, if you are using a machine, take care with the length of time the dough is kneaded. Always follow the manufacturers instructions and use a slow speed on the machine, at least until you are thoroughly familiar with the process.

4. Proving

If you are using fresh or ordinary dried yeast, the next step is the first proving time. This is to allow the yeast time to work and to give a well risen and even dough. After you have kneaded your dough, place it (or leave it) in a warm bowl and cover it with a clean tea cloth. Place the bowl in a warm area until the dough has doubled in size. This requirement has troubled many people who have sought out space in an airing cupboard or the like. In actual fact a well kneaded dough with the right ingredients will rise in most places of average temperature.

If you use fast acting yeast only one proving is necessary. If you use fresh or ordinary dried yeast, you will need to repeat the proving process after shaping.

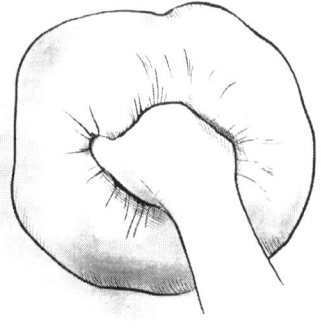

5. Knocking back

After this time has elapsed the dough must be 'knocked back'. This gets rid of any uneven pockets of air in the dough and restores the texture of the mixture. To 'knock back' simply take the dough out of the bowl, place it on the work surface and punch into the dough with your fist. It should not require much flour as it won't be sticky and too much extra flour will make the bread streaky. This is good for getting rid of any aggressive feelings you may be harbouring and it is also good for the bread! Knead it quickly for a few seconds till it has regained its shape.

6. Shaping

The next stage is the shaping of the dough. There are many traditional shapes of loaves that are fun to try and various shapes and sizes of tin. This is purely a matter of preference and choice but it is good to vary the shape of your bread depending on what you want to use the bread for once it is baked. For example, sandwiches are best made with bread baked in tins as it gives a more regular shape and homemade burgers are best eaten with flat type bread rolls. Once shaped it needs a warm place to rise before baking. Fast action yeast speeds up the proving time, so watch your dough. Don't just assume the time given in a recipe is correct. These are only guides and over proving the dough has certainly spoiled many loaves which can lose their shape and often tilt over.

See page 35 for more information on shaping your bread.

7. Finishing
Finishing a loaf generally comes just before or even during baking. This affects the finished crust. You can sprinkle the top with various seeds such as sesame, poppy or sunflower seeds and gently press them into the top of the loaf. This will give a crunchy topping to the bread. Oatmeal also gives an interesting finish to a loaf but isn't quite as crunchy for those who prefer a softer finish.

For a soft crust dust the dough with flour or brush it with vegetable oil. For a crispy crust brush the top of the bread with a salt-water mixture using half a teaspoon of salt to 4 tablespoons of hot water. Allow the mixture to cool before brushing it over the top of the dough.

Brushing with a teaspoon of sugar mixed with two tablespoons of milk will give a brown, crusty finish and egg and milk together will produce a shiny glaze on top of the finished loaf. Mix one egg with three tablespoons of milk and brush generously over the dough before cooking. This mixture will keep overnight in a refrigerator.

7. Baking
Baking the dough has two main purposes. The first and most obvious one is the cooking of the ingredients to make the bread edible. The second, and equally important purpose, is the killing of the yeast. Having your oven set to a high temperature does the latter. As yeast is very sensitive to high temperatures it is killed in the first few minutes of cooking, so some recipes may ask you to turn down the heat after a while so that the bread is not over baked. Most recipes, however, use a continuous high heat suitable for the size and type of loaf.

Testing the loaf is cooked
Testing if a loaf is cooked is usually down to the look and sound of the loaf. This may sound odd but the sound you get from a baked loaf is a very definite thudding sound when tapped on the bottom. If the loaf is in a tin it will need to be removed to do this. Use oven gloves at all times as the bread will be

incredibly hot. Turn the loaf over and tap the base with the palm of your hand. If it is cooked through it will produce a hollow, thudding noise.

The loaf should also be dark and golden in colour and, if cooked in a tin, should be slightly shrunken away from the sides. If the top of the loaf is cooking too quickly it may be in the wrong place in your oven, so alter its position by placing it on a lower shelf or turn the temperature down by a few degrees.

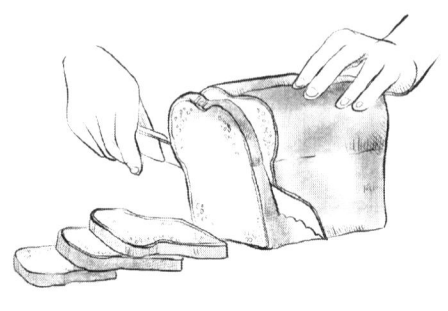

8. Cooling

When the bread is cooked, take it out of the tin or off the baking tray straight away and place it on a cooling rack as the crust will go soggy from the moisture emanating from the loaf. Cooling is a very important part of baking bread and, whereas small loaves are okay to be eaten warm, slicing too soon may actually spoil a larger loaf. Leave it to cool for at least 45 minutes before eating as slicing a hot loaf will squash its shape and the bread will lose its springy texture.

To recap, the basic stages in bread making are:

Using fresh or ordinary yeast	Using fast action yeast
Mixing	Mixing
Kneading	Kneading
Proving	Shaping
Knocking back	Proving
Shaping	Finishing
Proving	Baking
Finishing	Cooling
Baking	
Cooling	

Traditional bread shapes

The Bloomer
This is a long cob with diagonal cuts along the top of the bread. They can be any size to suit your taste and needs and are very easy to produce. It is good for slicing and large ones make reasonable shaped sandwiches.

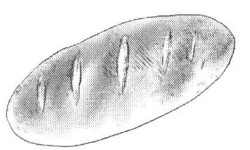

The Cottage Loaf
The dough is cut into two sections, one containing about two thirds of the dough. These two pieces are shaped into round balls and the base of the smaller section is moistened with water and placed on top of the larger ball. Then, using your index and middle fingers, push down through the centre of the top section through to the larger base. This will keep the two pieces together.

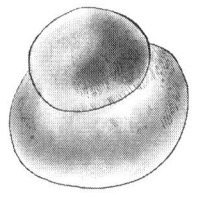

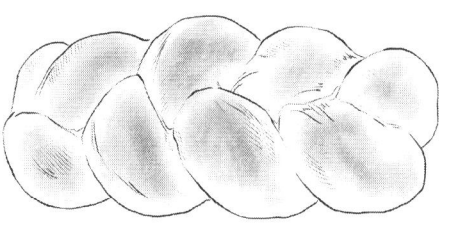

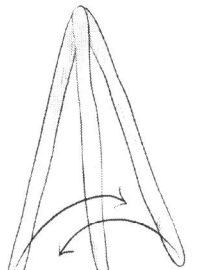

The Plait
Bread can be shaped into a three strand or a five strand plait. The latter makes a larger loaf sized plait that is good for slicing and the three strander is better for the smaller, single roll. Divide small sections of dough into threes and roll each section into thin sausage shapes. Squeeze three ends of the strands together and seal them with a little water. Plait the strands loosely and finally squeeze and moisten the other ends together in the same way as before.

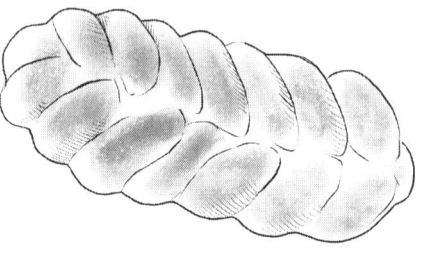 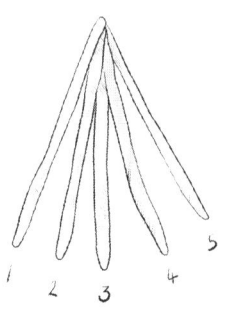

The five strander is a little more complicated. Divide the dough into five larger sausage shapes, moisten and squeeze the ends together and then spread the strands slightly apart. Number the strands 1 - 5 and follow this pattern, re-numbering the strands as you go along; 2 over 3, 5 over 2, 1 over 3. Continue the sequence until you reach the end of the strands. Moisten and squeeze together to seal the other ends as before.

This might sound complicated but the finished result is very impressive and gives an interesting shape to the sliced loaf.

The Tin Loaf

The traditional tin loaf is by far the easiest option. Shaping is very simple as when the dough rises it takes on the shape of whatever you have put it in. As long as they are well greased most baking tins make good containers for bread. Mould the amount of dough required for the tin, remembering that it will almost double in size during the proving time. Place it in the centre of the tin and leave it. It will mould itself as it rises.

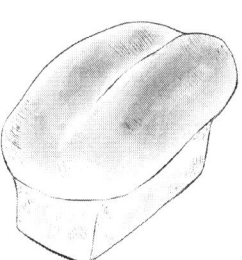

Split tin loaf

A split tin loaf is made by making a deep cut in the top of the dough about 15-20 minutes into the proving time, then leaving it to finish rising before baking.

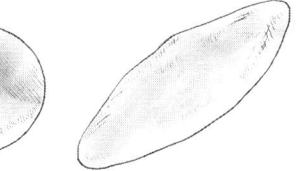

Individual Rolls

These are ideal for dinner parties, picnics, lunch boxes or to serve with soup or hors d'oeuvres. They can be round rolls or bridge rolls, which are more elongated in shape. Break off small amounts of dough and knead them into either a round or a sausage shape which tapers towards the ends. If you want to make your own burger buns, break off the required amount and form a round. As you place it on the sheet gently flatten it with the palm of your hand. The finished item will be a little flatter and ready to take a burger.

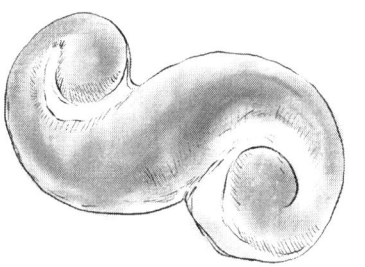

The Scroll

This is an interesting one. It is used as a fancy bread for special occasions and is a bit tricky to make, but looks good as a centre piece at a buffet party. The dough is rolled out fairly thickly into a basic triangle shape, then rolled from the wide end to the narrow tip giving a scroll effect. It is then left to prove for 15 minutes, brushed with egg and milk glaze, left for a further 10 minutes and then cooked.

Another way of making the scroll shape is to roll the dough into a rectangle and roll from one end half way then turn the dough over and roll from the other end making an 's' shape. This is then left to prove like the first example and finished in the same way.

The Wheatsheaf

At harvest time celebrations a traditional 'wheatsheaf' is made out of dough. This is a large, ornate, flat loaf in the shape of a sheaf of wheat that is often used as the centre of a harvest display. It is usually made by the local professional baker.

Chapter Four

Family Bread Recipes

The majority of these recipes are the traditional loaves that are consumed daily in most households. I've tried to include all the basic recipes using each variety of yeast and the many flour types that are now readily available. Some are easy but others are a little more complicated and these may require a little experience. The first recipe is the quickest and easiest type of bread to make and is ideal when you want fresh bread fast. It contains no yeast so there is no proving or kneading necessary.

Soda Bread

 DIFFICULTY
Easy

 PREP TIME 20 mins
BAKE TIME 20-25 mins

This bread tastes wonderful a few minutes after baking and, unlike yeasted bread, will not give you indigestion so soon after baking because of its soda content. I usually serve this with homemade soups or cheese and pickles for lunch. It isn't possible to make a conventional sandwich with it because of its crumbly texture but, once cool, is ideal for an open sandwich. Soda bread needs to be eaten on the same day that it is baked, but this shouldn't be a problem once you have tasted it. In our house it rarely cools before it is gobbled up! This recipe requires buttermilk which can be bought from the supermarket, or you can make your own as described in the final chapter.

INGREDIENTS

450 g self-raising flour

1 level teaspoon salt

1 level teaspoon baking powder

284 ml/10 fl oz carton buttermilk

1. Preheat the oven to 220ºC/Gas mark 7 and grease a baking tray with a little oil
2. Sift the flour, salt and baking powder together in a large mixing bowl.
3. Stir in the buttermilk and bind to a soft dough. The mixture should be a little sticky. If the mixture seems too dry add a little more milk or water.
4. Form into a round and place on a baking tray.
5. Cut diagonally across the top of the loaf to make four sections.
6. Bake for 20-25 minutes until golden brown.

Variations on a theme

Oaty Soda Bread

This is my personal favourite as it has the addition of health giving oats. Use 350g/12 oz flour and 100g/4 oz of medium rolled oats. The other ingredients are the same as the previous recipe, but after step 2, stir in the oats. Finish as in the basic recipe.

Cheese Soda Bread

After mixing all the dry ingredients, add 50g/2/oz of grated mature cheddar to the mixture before adding the buttermilk. Continue as in the basic method.

You may also add fresh or dried herbs to the mixture. I like to add half a teaspoon of fresh or dried thyme to the recipe before mixing in the liquid ingredient.

Chopped, sun-dried tomatoes or olives are another delicious addition, but do be careful to drain all the oil or brine from the ones that come in a jar.

Simple White Loaf

DIFFICULTY
Easy

PREP TIME   Approx 1 hour
BAKE TIME   30-40 mins

This recipe is the least complicated bread to make using yeast and will make two medium sized loaves.

INGREDIENTS

900 g/2 lb. strong white flour

2 level teaspoons salt

1 sachet fast action dried yeast

1 tablespoon sunflower oil

Approximately 568 ml/ 1 pint warm water

1. Sieve the flour and salt into a large bowl and stir in the yeast.
2. Make a well in the centre of the flour and add the oil and water, mixing well with a wooden spoon.
3. Use your hands to finish combining the flour and water and begin kneading in the bowl.
4. Transfer the dough, if you wish, to a lightly floured surface and knead for 10 minutes. Alternatively keep kneading in the bowl.
5. Shape the dough into your preferred shape and place in oiled tins or on baking trays and leave to prove until doubled in size. This will take approximately 35-45 minutes in a warm place.
6. Bake at 220ºC/Gas mark 7 for 30-40 minutes.

Helpful hint
The two recipes on page 42-43 can be made with brown, wholemeal or a mixture of white, wholemeal and brown flour, substituting the amounts as necessary. Wholemeal flour needs a little more liquid than white flour so you will need to adjust the amounts of liquid, adding 20 ml extra if using wholemeal on its own.

White Bread
Using Fresh or Dried Yeast

 DIFFICULTY
Easy

 PREP TIME 90 mins
BAKE TIME 30-40 mins

This recipe is simple, though there are a number of steps involved, and makes 3 medium sized loaves.

INGREDIENTS

1.4 kg/3 lb. strong white flour

4 level teaspoons salt

25 g/1 oz fresh yeast or 15 g/ 1/2 oz dried yeast

2 teaspoons sugar (to mix with the yeast)

2 tablespoons sunflower oil

1 tablespoon sugar

900 ml/ 1 1/2 pints warm water

1. Crumble the fresh yeast into the warm water or mix the dried yeast with half of the warm water. Add the 2 teaspoons of sugar. Leave for 15 minutes in a warm place until frothy.
2. Sieve the flour and salt together in a large bowl and make a well in the centre.
3. Add the yeast mixture, the extra water if using dried yeast, the oil and the other sugar.
4. Mix well with a wooden spoon, then finish combining the ingredients by hand.
5. Knead until the mixture forms a smooth ball, transferring to a lightly floured surface and knead for a further 10 minutes.
6. Place the dough in a very lightly oiled bowl, cover with a clean tea cloth and leave to prove till the dough has doubled in size.
7. Knock back the dough and knead for a further 5 minutes. Shape the dough into the desired shape and place in an oiled tin or on an oiled baking tray and leave to prove again until doubled in size.
8. Bake at 220ºC/Gas mark 7 for 30-40 minutes.

Quick Granary Loaf

DIFFICULTY
Easy

PREP TIME 60 mins
BAKE TIME 30-40 mins

Granary flour is now widely available and makes a tasty filling bread. It gives a very nutty flavour to the loaf.

INGREDIENTS

450 g/1 lb. white strong flour

450 g/1 lb. granary flour

1 sachet fast action dried yeast

568 ml/1 pint warm water but a little more may be required depending on the flour

1 tablespoon sunflower oil

2 level teaspoons salt

1. Sieve the two flours and salt into a large bowl and stir in the yeast.
2. Make a well in the centre of the flour and add the oil and water, mixing well with a wooden spoon.
3. Use your hands to finish combining the flour and water and begin kneading in the bowl.
4. Transfer the dough, if you wish, to a lightly floured surface and knead for 10 minutes. Alternatively keep kneading in the bowl.
5. Shape the dough into your preferred shape and place in oiled tins or on baking trays and leave to prove until doubled in size. This will take approximately 35-45 minutes in a warm place.
6. Bake at 220ºC/Gas mark 7 for 30-40 minutes.

Milk Loaf

DIFFICULTY
Easy

PREP TIME 55 mins
BAKE TIME 30-35 mins

Milk bread is a great alternative to ordinary white bread. It is very soft but makes wonderfully crispy toast. The following recipe is sufficient for one loaf.

INGREDIENTS

450 g/1 lb. strong
white flour

1 level teaspoon salt

1 sachet fast action
dried yeast

275 ml/ 1/2 pint warm
whole milk

1. Sieve the flour and salt into a large bowl and stir in the yeast, making a well in the centre of the flour.
2. Gradually stir in the warm milk and combine by hand into a ball, kneading for 10 minutes until smooth.
3. Shape into a large roll and place on an oiled baking sheet and leave to prove until doubled in size.
4. Bake for 30-35 minutes at 220ºC/Gas mark 7.

Oatmeal Bread

 DIFFICULTY
Easy

 PREP TIME 55 mins
BAKE TIME 25-30 mins

This is one of my family's favourites. The oats give an added nutty taste and they also have significant health benefits too.

INGREDIENTS

700 g/ 1 1/2 lb. strong white flour

200 g/8 oz fine oatmeal

1 sachet fast action dried yeast

2 teaspoons salt

Approximately 568 ml/ 1 pint warm water

1 tablespoon sunflower oil

1. Sieve the flour and salt into a bowl and stir in the oats and yeast.
2. Make a well in the centre, add the water and oil and stir.
3. Use your hands to combine the ingredients and form into a ball.
4. Knead for 10 minutes until smooth.
5. Divide the mixture into two and form into rounds. Leave to prove till doubled in size.
6. Bake for 25-30 minutes at 220ºC/Gas mark 7.

Old Fashioned Herb Bread

 DIFFICULTY
Easy

 PREP TIME 60 mins
BAKE TIME 30-35 mins

This loaf has a very different texture to other breads. It is very soft and has an open texture that makes it ideal served with patés and soft cheese. You can use whichever herbs you prefer or a grand mixture so that each mouthful tastes slightly different. Good herb mixtures are tarragon and parsley or marjoram and thyme. Sage and chives gives a good savoury flavour too. If you use these herbs only add 1 tablespoon of fresh and 1 teaspoon of dried. Use two 1 lb. tins if you want a smaller loaf for serving with paté as a starter and bake for 5-10 minutes less than the last part of the method.

INGREDIENTS

350 g/12 oz strong white flour

1 large beaten egg

1 tablespoon sunflower oil

1/2 sachet fast action dried yeast

225 ml/8 fl oz warm milk

1 1/2 teaspoons salt

2 tablespoons finely chopped herbs or 1.5 teaspoons dried herbs of your choice

Fennel or poppy seeds for sprinkling on the top

1. Sieve the salt and flour together into a bowl and stir in the yeast.
2. Combine the egg and milk in a jug and pour into the centre of the flour, leaving a little to brush the top of the loaf before baking.
3. Add the oil and herbs you are using and mix well with a wooden spoon. Add a little more flour if the mixture is too sticky, but only teaspoon by teaspoon so that you don't add to much.
4. Use your hands to combine the ingredients into a ball and knead for 10 minutes.
5. Shape so that the dough fits into an oiled 2 lb. loaf tin and leave to prove until either doubled in size or standing slightly proud of the top of the tin.
6. Gently brush the top with the leftover egg and milk mixture and sprinkle your loaf with your choice of seeds.
7. Bake for 30-35 minutes at 210ºC/Gas mark 6.

Potato Bread

 **DIFFICULTY**
Easy

 PREP TIME Approx 1 hour
BAKE TIME 30-45 mins

Potato bread is filling and nutritious. It makes a real treat on those cold days, especially when eaten with warming soups. This recipe makes one large loaf or two smaller cobs. If using a tin this corresponds to a 2 lb. or two 1 lb. tins.

INGREDIENTS

1 medium sized potato, approx. 5-6 oz in weight

500 g/1 lb. 2 oz strong white flour

2 teaspoons salt

250 ml/8 fl oz warm milk

1 egg

1 sachet fast action dried yeast

3 tablespoons creme fraiche

1. Grate the raw potato into a large bowl.
2. Pour over the warm milk and add the yeast.
3. Sieve the flour and salt together in a separate bowl and gradually beat half the flour into the potato mixture.
4. Beat in the egg and creme fraiche and follow with the rest of the flour.
5. Knead the dough for 10 minutes and shape.
6. Place in oiled tins and prove for 40 minutes.
7. When doubled in size, bake at 180ºC/Gas mark 5 for 45 minutes or 30-35 minutes if smaller loaves have been made.

Onion Bread

 DIFFICULTY
Easy

 PREP TIME 1 hour
BAKE TIME 25-30mins

Another tasty, savoury bread is made with onions gently fried till they begin to caramelise. I prefer to make this into long flat rolls to be served with soup or salads, or try toasting them with cheese on the top. Delicious!

INGREDIENTS

500 g/1 lb. 2 oz strong white flour

2 teaspoons salt

1 sachet fast action dried yeast

280-300 ml/ 1/2 pint warm water

1 tablespoon sunflower oil

FOR THE ONION TOPPING

2 small onions finely sliced

50 g/2 oz butter

2 level tablespoons plain flour

150 ml/5 fl oz milk

1 chopped clove garlic (optional)

1/2 level teaspoon salt

Black pepper to taste

Onion seeds to sprinkle on top

1. Make the bread as per the simple white bread recipe, place on a baking tray and flatten well by hand or with a rolling pin. Leave to prove for 30 minutes.
2. Meanwhile, fry the onions gently in the butter, adding the garlic if using.
3. Continue to cook until the onions begin to caramelise.
4. Sprinkle over the flour and mix well into the onions.
5. Gradually add the milk, stirring all the time and keeping the heat low so the mixture doesn't burn.
6. Bring to the boil then simmer for a few seconds, adding salt and pepper.
7. After the bread has finished proving, spread the onion mixture over the top and sprinkle with the onion seeds.
8. Bake for 25-30 minutes at 200ºC/Gas mark 6.

Tomato Bread

 DIFFICULTY
Easy

 PREP TIME 45 mins
BAKE TIME 30-40 mins

This is a very unusual and great flavoured bread that I saw on one of Keith Floyd's television programmes. Over the years I have added different ingredients and have changed the recipe. Have a go at this one but try adding your own favourite ingredients.

INGREDIENTS

750 g/1 lb. 8 oz strong white flour

Can of tomatoes, drained and chopped (use the remaining liquid in a pasta sauce)

1 tablespoon tomato puree

1 sachet fast action dried yeast

1 level teaspoon salt

1 level tablespoon sugar

1 tablespoon olive oil

80 ml/3 oz warm water or the warmed tomato liquor

1. Sieve the flour and salt into a large bowl and stir in the yeast and sugar.
2. Add the warm liquid, tomatoes, oil and tomato puree.
3. Mix well with a wooden spoon and then use your hands to finish combining and knead for 10 minutes.
4. Place in a well oiled 2 lb. loaf tin and prove for 30-35 minutes in a warm place.
5. Bake for 30-40 minutes at 220ºC/Gas mark 7.

Helpful hint Try adding some basil or oregano to the dry ingredients for a mediterranean flavour

Individual Rolls

 DIFFICULTY
Easy

 PREP TIME 60 mins
BAKE TIME 30-40 mins

Individual rolls are great to serve at dinner parties. They don't keep as well as larger loaves but if kept in an airtight container rather than a bread bin they will last a little longer. The following recipe makes approximately 18 rolls. You can vary the batch by making different shapes and finishing them with a variety of seeds such as poppy, onion, sesame or fennel on top of each roll.

INGREDIENTS

700 g/1 lb. 8 oz strong white or brown flour

2 teaspoons salt

1 sachet fast action dried yeast

1 tablespoon sunflower oil

450 ml/ 3/4 pint warm water

1. Sieve the salt and flour together into a bowl.
2. Add the yeast and stir well.
3. Pour the water into the centre of the flour and add the oil.
4. Mix with a wooden spoon and use your hands to combine into a ball.
5. Knead for 10 minutes and break the dough into 18 small pieces and shape as required.
6. Place on an oiled baking sheet a few centimetres apart and leave to prove for 30 minutes.
7. Bake for 15-20 minutes at 220ºC/Gas mark 7.

Rye Bread

DIFFICULTY
Easy

PREP TIME 45 mins
BAKE TIME 25-35 mins

This is a really nutty bread with a deep flavour and a very satisfying texture. The following recipe is one that my grandma used to make. She would prepare granddads' packed lunch with this because she said it filled him up for longer. He still came home ravenous, though.

INGREDIENTS

300 g/10 1/2 oz rye flour

200 g/7 oz strong white flour

300 g/10 1/2 oz oats

3 teaspoons salt

25 g/1 0z fresh yeast

250 ml/8 fl oz warm water

1 teaspoon sugar

1. Crumble the fresh yeast into the water and add the sugar.
2. Mix all the dry ingredients together in a large bowl.
3. Add the yeast mixture and combine with your hands until it forms a ball. Add a little more warm water if the dough feels too stiff.
4. Knead in the bowl for 5 minutes then transfer to a lightly floured surface and knead for a further 5 minutes.
5. Return to the bowl and cover with a clean tea towel. Leave to prove for 30 minutes.
6. Knock back and knead for a few more minutes, then shape and place in a lightly oiled 2 lb. loaf tin and leave to prove for another 30 minutes.
7. Bake for 25-35 minutes at 200ºC/Gas mark 6.

Mixed Seed Bread

 DIFFICULTY
Easy

 PREP TIME 45 mins
BAKE TIME 25-35 mins

You can now buy flours ready mixed with seeds but I prefer to add my own in the quantities my family enjoys. It is easy to find many small packs containing all kinds of seeds and this makes it easy to bake a variety of bread with interesting textures. I have found that even the most hardened white bread eaters enjoy the taste of seeded bread. The next recipe is a quick and easy mixed seed bread.

INGREDIENTS

800 g/ 1 lb. 7 oz strong white flour (or half and half with brown flour)

2 sachets fast action dried yeast

1 tablespoon sunflower oil

3 teaspoons salt

125 g/4 1/2 oz mixed seeds of your choice (try linseed, poppy, pumpkin, sesame or sunflower)

280 ml/8 fl oz warm water

1. Mix all the dry ingredients together in a large bowl.
2. Make a well in the centre of the flour and add water and oil. Mix together with a wooden spoon.
3. Use your hands to combine the ingredients and form a ball. Knead for 10 minutes.
4. Shape into a round or oval loaf and place on an oiled baking sheet.
5. Leave in a warm place until it has doubled in size.
6. Extra seeds may be sprinkled on the top of the loaf before baking. Brush the top with a little water before sprinkling on the seeds.
7. Bake for 25-35 minutes at 220ºC/Gas mark 7.

Muesli Bread

DIFFICULTY
Easy

PREP TIME 55 mins
BAKE TIME 30-35 mins

This is an excellent breakfast bread. It is great toasted with lots of butter. It is best made with unsweetened or low sugar muesli as the flavour is better and it can easily become too sweet.

INGREDIENTS

180 g/6 oz muesli, either with fruit or both fruit and nuts

900 g/1 1/2 lb. strong white flour

1 sachet fast action dried yeast

50 g/2 oz raisins

50 g/2 oz melted butter

450 ml/ 3/4 pint warm water

1 teaspoon salt

1. Sieve the flour and salt together and stir in the yeast.
2. Add the water and butter and mix well.
3. Knead for 10 minutes and place in 2 well oiled loaf tins.
4. Leave to prove for 40 minutes.
5. Bake 30-35 minutes at 200ºC/Gas mark 6.

Breakfast Muffins

 DIFFICULTY
Easy

 PREP TIME 50 mins
COOK TIME 10-15 mins/batch

Breakfast muffins and crumpets are a real favourite in our house and are easy to make. You can cook them in a heavy-based frying pan but a griddle pan is best.

INGREDIENTS

275 g/10 oz strong white flour

2 level teaspoons salt

220 ml/8 fl oz warm water

1/2 sachet fast action dried yeast

1 tablespoon sunflower oil

1. Sieve the flour and salt into a bowl and stir in the yeast.
2. Make a well in the centre of the flour and pour in the water and oil.
3. Combine all the ingredients until a soft dough is formed. It should still hold its shape but be much softer and more difficult to handle than normal dough.
4. Knead the sticky dough for at least 7 minutes and leave to prove in a warm place for 40 minutes.
5. Heat a griddle pan that has been lightly oiled until hot.
6. Break off small sections of the dough and make flat rounds. Cook 3-4 at a time on the griddle, turning down the heat to medium so the crust doesn't burn.
7. Cook for 10-12 minutes, turning the muffin over after 5-6 minutes. Keep each batch warm in the oven until ready to serve.
8. Serve warm with butter. Tear the muffins apart rather than cutting them with a knife.

Pikelets and Crumpets

 DIFFICULTY
Easy

 PREP TIME 55 mins
COOK TIME 3-5 mins/batch

I find it better to use fresh yeast in this recipe as the bubbles form more successfully when the crumpet or pikelet is cooking. There is no kneading to be done but the yeast mixture needs time to ferment to produce the bubbles. Crumpets are cooked in the same way as muffins but use a metal ring to keep the mixture in place. Pikelets are made on the griddle without the ring.

INGREDIENTS

225 g/8 oz strong white flour

1 level teaspoon salt

15 g/ 1/2 oz fresh yeast

1/2 teaspoon sugar

150 ml/ 1/4 pint warm water

150 ml/ 1/4 pint warm milk

1/4 teaspoon bicarbonate of soda

1 egg white, beaten until frothy

4 tablespoons cold water

1. Sieve the flour and salt together into a large bowl.
2. Mix together the milk and water and crumble in the yeast. Add the sugar and stir.
3. Pour the yeast mixture into the flour and beat vigorously for 5-6 minutes. The batter must be covered and left in a warm place for 30-40 minutes.
4. Dissolve the bicarbonate of soda in the cold water and beat lightly into the batter.
5. Fold in the egg white making sure it is thoroughly combined into the batter.
6. If cooking pikelets, use a ladle to spoon some mixture onto a hot, oiled griddle. Turn the pikelet over when the surface is looking dry. This is only a few seconds each side. Don't overcook them as they can lose flavour.
7. Keep each pikelet warm while cooking the rest of the batter. Either eat hot from the pan with butter or honey or toast them when cold. They will keep till the following day.
8. If cooking crumpets, use a metal ring on the griddle. Allow to cook until the top looks 'set'. Cook on one side only and serve toasted.

Breadsticks

 DIFFICULTY
Easy

 PREP TIME 30 mins
BAKE TIME 8-10 mins

Breadsticks can be eaten with many types of dip and soups. They are great for parties and adding cheese, herbs and seeds will vary the flavour. Breadsticks are really easy to make and taste so much better than the shop bought variety.

INGREDIENTS

225 g/8 oz
self-raising flour

1 dessert spoon sugar

1 rounded teaspoon salt

125 ml/4 fl oz milk

Melted butter to dip the
fingers in, about 20 g/1 oz

1. Mix all the dry ingredients together.
2. Add the milk and mix well.
3. Knead to form a pliable dough and then roll into a rectangle about 1.5 cm thick and cut into strips, each one about 1 cm wide and 12-15 cm long.
4. Dip each strip into melted butter and place on an oiled baking sheet.
5. Bake at 200°C/Gas mark 6 for 8 - 10 minutes, or until golden brown.

Variations on a theme

Cheese Breadsticks
This is the same recipe as above but you add 50 g/2 oz strong cheddar to the dry ingredients before adding the milk and continue in the same way.

Herb Breadsticks
Add 1 teaspoon of dried herbs or 1 tablespoon of mixed seeds of your choice to the dry ingredients and follow the recipe as described above.

Chapter Five

Bread Recipes From Around The World

Thankfully specialist breads from all over the world can now be purchased in delicatessens, supermarkets and farmers markets everywhere. But do have a go at making your own. They are certainly much easier than you think. The following is only a small selection of the variety of breads from all over the world. I am sure I have missed out many others, but the list will give you a broad understanding of cooking with yeast and will hopefully prompt you to go on to further develop your skills in the craft of bread making.

Naan

 DIFFICULTY
Easy

 PREP TIME 30 mins
BAKE TIME 3-4 mins

I thought I wouldn't be able to make a naan as I didn't have a tandoor oven to cook in, but my friend, Nusrut, is Kashmiri and makes them in her conventional oven. This recipe is the one Nusrut makes regularly for her family.

Naan is a wonderfully soft, almost creamy tasting bread that is traditionally baked in a tandoor, pressed onto the side of the oven and cooked at a very high temperature so that bubbles form in the dough. It is cooked very quickly, which keeps it soft and moist. It can be cooked in a regular oven so long as it reaches a temperature of 230ºC/Gas mark 8. The following recipe is sufficient to serve 6 people as an accompaniment or 3 people if it is the main carbohydrate portion of a meal.

INGREDIENTS

225 g/8 oz strong white flour

1/2 teaspoon salt

1 sachet yeast

4 tablespoons warm milk

1 tablespoon sunflower oil

2 tablespoons plain yoghurt

1 egg, beaten

1. Mix together the flour, salt and yeast into a bowl.
2. Add the milk, oil, yoghurt and the beaten egg.
3. Knead for 10 minutes and leave to prove for 30 minutes.
4. Towards the end of the proving time, heat an oiled baking sheet in a hot oven at 230ºC/Gas mark 8.
5. Divide into 3 sections and roll out into the traditional teardrop shape. Place on the hot baking sheet and put it in the hottest part of your oven for 3-4 minutes.

Bread Recipes From Around The World 61

Chapatis

 DIFFICULTY
Easy

 PREP TIME 20 mins
BAKE TIME 1-2 mins/chapati

Chapatis are traditionally cooked on a tava. This is a cast iron plate but they are also easily made using a large, heavy base frying pan or a griddle and cooked lightly on both sides.

It is best to make them in batches, keeping the baked ones warm until the whole batch is cooked. These flat, unleavened rounds are made from atta flour which is made from wheat using the germ and the endosperm but not the bran. Your local Asian food store will have atta flour but many supermarkets are now beginning to stock it as well. If you cannot find atta flour then wholemeal is fine. This recipe makes approximately 8 chapatis.

INGREDIENTS

---

225 g/8 oz atta or
wholemeal flour

150-180 ml/5-7 fl oz
water

1/2 teaspoon salt

1. Place the flour in a bowl and add the water, combining them slowly with a wooden spoon.
2. Knead lightly until the dough is pliable.
3. Heat the pan over a medium heat.
4. Divide the dough into 8 pieces and knead into a ball. Roll out on a lightly floured surface until approximately 20 cm/8 inch in diameter.
5. Shake off any excess flour and place in the hot frying pan, cooking for a minute or so then turn over and cook on the other side.

Variations on a theme

Poori
You can make poori in a very similar way to chapatis by just adding 2 tablespoons of sunflower oil and reducing the water by 30 ml. Roll out in the same way as chapatis but cook in a little vegetable oil about 1 cm deep. If the

poori start to float, keep pressing them under the oil until they are light and puffy in texture. Turn the poori over for a few seconds and then place on some kitchen paper to get rid of excess oil. Keep warm if not being served straight away or they will lose their crispness.

Aloo Parathas

 **DIFFICULTY**
Easy

 PREP TIME 40 mins
BAKE TIME 3-4 mins/item

Potato parathas are my favourite accompaniment to Asian food. They are very tasty and I enjoy using them to pick up my food. They are a filling and satisfying bread when hungry.

INGREDIENTS

400 g/14 oz wheatmeal flour

1 teaspoon sugar

1 teaspoon salt
230 ml/8 fl oz milk or water

1 egg, beaten

4 medium potatoes, boiled and mashed

2 tablespoons finely chopped fresh coriander

30-40 g/1-2 oz ghee for frying

1. Mix the flour, sugar and salt together in a bowl.
2. Add the beaten egg and milk and combine to form a dough. Knead until smooth.
3. Combine the mashed potato and coriander with a little extra seasoning to taste.
4. Divide the dough into 6 equal balls and roll out to form a flat disc.
5. Place a tablespoon of potato mixture into the centre of the dough.
6. Bring up the edges and moisten with a little water so that the dough sticks together. Twist the edges and flatten down.
7. Finally turn the paratha over and roll flat.
8. Heat a griddle or frying pan with a generous amount of ghee. Place a paratha twist side down in the pan and cook for a few minutes.
9. Brush the top with more ghee and turn over to cook the other side in the same way until both sides are golden brown.

Pitta Bread

 DIFFICULTY
Easy

 PREP TIME 50 mins
BAKE TIME 5-8 mins

Pitta bread originates in the Middle East, but is now widely popular mainly because of the way they break open and are easily filled with salads, kebabs or anything else you fancy. This recipe makes 8-10 pieces.

INGREDIENTS

450 g/1 lb. strong white flour

1 sachet fast action dried yeast

1 teaspoon salt

300 ml/ 1/2 pint warm water

1. Sieve the flour and salt together into a bowl.
2. Stir in the yeast.
3. Make a well in the centre and pour in the water.
4. Combine well to form a soft dough.
5. Knead for 10 minutes until smooth and leave to prove for 20 minutes.
6. Break the dough into 8-10 equal pieces.
7. Roll out each piece into an oval shape about 4 mm/ 1/3 inch thick, place on a baking tray and leave to rest for 8-10 minutes.
8. Bake in the oven at the hottest temperature (at least 230ºC/Gas mark 8) for 5-8 minutes until puffed up and golden.

Bread Recipes From Around The World

Chinese Pan Bread

 DIFFICULTY
Easy

 PREP TIME 25 mins
COOK TIME 2-3 mins

Chinese pan bread can be served with any type of food. I enjoy them with a poached egg on top.

INGREDIENTS

225 g/8 oz plain flour

175 ml/7 fl oz water

5 finely chopped spring onions

2 teaspoons sunflower oil

1 teaspoon salt

1. Combine the onions and oil.
2. Sieve the flour and salt together and gradually pour in the water whilst mixing well.
3. Knead for a few minutes until the dough is smooth.
4. Add the onion mixture to the dough and knead again until well combined.
5. Divide into 4 equal pieces and knead each piece.
6. Roll into 1 cm thick rounds and fry each round in a little oil.

Injera

DIFFICULTY
Easy

PREP TIME 10 mins
COOK TIME 2 mins

Injera are a cross between a pancake and a flatbread. They are very quick to make and you can cook a lot in a short space of time. They go really well with thick stews and curries as you can scoop up the food with them as you would with a fork or spoon. They come from Ethiopia and are made from a type of flour called 'teff' that contains practically no gluten. Ordinary plain wheat flour may be substituted to make these.

INGREDIENTS

---

300 g/10 oz plain flour,
brown or white

450 ml/12 fl oz water

1/2 teaspoon salt

1. Mix the flour. salt and water together and beat vigorously to a smooth batter.
2. Fry in a little oil in a hot frying pan, adding enough of the batter to coat the bottom of the pan. Slightly thicker than a crepe is about the correct thickness for injera.
3. Cook until the upper-side is dry. There is no need to turn them over as they will already be thoroughly cooked.

Coconut Bread

 DIFFICULTY
Easy

 PREP TIME 10 mins
BAKE TIME 25-30 mins

This wonderful bread from Africa is delicious toasted for breakfast and topped with marmalade or jam.

INGREDIENTS

500 g/1 lb 2 oz plain flour

2 teaspoons baking powder

100 g/4 oz melted butter

130 ml/4 1/2 fl oz milk or coconut milk

150 g/5 oz grated coconut

175 g/6 oz sugar

1 egg, beaten

1/2 teaspoon salt

1. Sift together the dry ingredients and stir in the sugar.
2. Add the coconut and make a well in the centre of the flour. Pour in the liquid, melted butter and beaten egg.
3. Mix together thoroughly and knead with your hands for a few minutes.
4. Place in 2 lb. or two 1 lb. oiled loaf tins.
5. Score the top and brush with a little water and sprinkle with sugar.
6. Bake for 25-30 minutes at 190°C/Gas mark 5 until golden brown. Leave to cool completely before slicing

Bagels

DIFFICULTY
Easy

PREP TIME 55 mins
COOK TIME 15 mins

Although originally Yiddish and eastern European in origin, it is the American market which has popularised the bagel. They are now readily available in most shops and supermarkets. These ring shaped rolls are boiled before baking. They seem a little messy to make but taste so good. My daughter loves them filled with cream cheese and smoked salmon. Very decadent! The following recipe makes 18-20 bagels.

INGREDIENTS

500 g/1 lb. strong white flour

250 ml/9 fl oz warm water

1 sachet fast action dried yeast

6 teaspoons caster sugar

1 teaspoon salt

2 tablespoons sunflower oil

2 eggs, beaten lightly

1. Mix the flour, sugar, salt and yeast together in a bowl.
2. Make a well in the centre of the flour and pour in the water, oil and eggs, keeping a few teaspoons of the egg back to glaze the bagels.
3. Stir well and combine by hand. Knead the dough for 10 minutes until smooth.
4. Roll into a ball, cover and leave to prove for 15 minutes.
5. Knead again for a few minutes and shape sections of dough into rings, moistening the edges to be pinched together. Leave on a floured surface to prove for 30 minutes covered with a towel.
6. Preheat the oven to 200ºC/Gas mark 6.
7. Meanwhile, poach the bagels in slightly salted boiling water for 15-20 seconds. Drain well and place on an oiled baking tray.
8. Brush with the egg glaze and bake for 10-15 minutes.

Bread Recipes From Around The World

Classic Cornbread

 DIFFICULTY
Easy

 PREP TIME 15 mins
BAKE TIME 30-40 mins

This is a basic cornbread recipe. Other ingredients can be added to vary the taste, but the main recipe remains the same and is very easy to make.

INGREDIENTS

140 g/5 oz cornmeal (semolina)

125 g/4 oz plain white flour

1 teaspoon baking soda

2 eggs

115 g/3 1/2 oz butter

235 ml/8 fl oz buttermilk

1 level teaspoon salt

1 tablespoon sugar

1. Melt the butter with the sugar in a large pan over a low heat.
2. Beat in the eggs.
3. Stir in the baking soda and buttermilk.
4. Beat in the flour and salt to make a smooth batter.
5. Pour the batter into a well oiled 20 cm/8 inch square tin.
6. Bake for 30-40 minutes at 180ºC/Gas mark 4.

Variations on a theme

If you like it sweet
Add 2 tablespoons of sugar, 50 g/2 oz of raisins or sultanas, a level teaspoon of cinnamon and a sprinkle of grated nutmeg.

If you like it hot
Add 2 chopped jalapeño chillies or even more if you like it *really* hot.

If you like cheese
Add 1/2 teaspoon of dry mustard and 50 g of grated strong cheddar or Monterey Jack cheese. Sprinkle extra cheese on top when just out of the oven.

Corn Tortillas

 DIFFICULTY
Easy

PREP TIME 15 mins
COOK TIME 2 mins/tortilla

Tortillas are the most popular bread of Mexico and are traditionally made with maize flour. They can be eaten with most foods, especially chilli based meat and vegetable dishes. Here are two recipes, one using the traditional maize flour and the other using ordinary plain flour. The two recipes make 10-12 large tortillas.

INGREDIENTS

450 g/1 lb. maize flour

175 g/6 oz plain white flour

1 teaspoon salt

600 ml/1 pint hot water

1. Mix the flours and salt together and slowly add the hot water.
2. Knead for 5 minutes till smooth. Add more flour or water to get the right consistency that is pliable and easy to use.
3. Divide the mixture into 10-12 pieces and roll each one into a large disc that will fit into your frying pan.
4. Heat your pan with a small amount of oil and fry each side for a minute each side.
5. Store in the fridge wrapped in a clean, damp cloth until needed and warm in a hot frying pan when ready to serve.

Bread Recipes From Around The World 71

Flour Tortillas

 DIFFICULTY
Easy

 PREP TIME 15 mins
COOK TIME 2 mins/tortilla

This recipe for tortillas is lighter and good for wraps.

INGREDIENTS

500 g/1 lb. plain flour

1 teaspoon salt

300 ml/9 fl oz warm water

2 tablespoons sunflower oil

1. Sieve the flour and salt together into a bowl and add the water and oil.
2. Mix well to form a ball.
3. Knead for 4-5 minutes until the dough is no longer sticky.
4. Divide the dough into 10-12 equal parts and roll each piece into a large disc as thin as manageable. Fry in a non-stick pan for a minute on both sides and pile up each tortilla on a large plate.
5. Serve warm or cool and freeze until needed. Thaw completely before reheating in a hot frying pan.

Blinis

DIFFICULTY
Easy

PREP TIME 50 mins
COOK TIME 2-3 mins/blini

Blinis are an ancient Russian pancake made from buckwheat. They can be served at breakfast or as a starter course with smoked salmon or caviar. We like to eat them with bacon and scrambled eggs.

Make as many as you can eat fresh as they don't store well. The following recipe makes 12-15 blinis and uses buckwheat flour. If you have difficulty finding it, use wholewheat flour instead.

INGREDIENTS

90 g/3 oz buckwheat flour

60 g/2 oz plain flour

1 sachet fast action dried yeast

300 ml/10 fl oz water or 1/2 milk and 1/2 water, warmed

2 eggs, separated

1/2 teaspoon salt

60 g/2 oz melted butter

120 ml/4 fl oz soured cream

1. Sieve the flour and salt into a large bowl and stir in the yeast.
2. Make a well in the centre of the flour and pour in the warm liquid, melted butter and egg yolks.
3. Whisk together to make a smooth batter and add cream. Whisk this in lightly.
4. Leave the batter in a warm place for 45 minutes until very frothy.
5. Whisk the egg whites until firm and fold into the batter mixture.
6. Heat a large frying pan or griddle lightly oiled by wiping a piece of oiled kitchen paper over the cooking surface of the pan.
7. When hot, ladle a little of the batter into the pan to make small pancakes.
8. Cook for a minute or so until golden, then turn the blini over and cook for a further minute.
9. Keep them warm in an oven whilst cooking the rest of the batch.

Limpa Bread

 DIFFICULTY
Easy

 PREP TIME 1 hour
BAKE TIME 30-35 mins

Swedish Limpa bread is a very rich, heavy bread which is good to eat in the winter time when appetites are hearty. It is delicious sliced and served with butter or marmalade. It keeps well in an air-tight container and is equally good toasted.

INGREDIENTS

700 g/1 1/2 lb. rye flour

175 g/6 oz strong white flour

2 tablespoons dried yeast

1 teaspoon sugar

550 ml/1 pint warm milk

90 g/3 oz melted butter

1 teaspoon salt

4 tablespoons golden syrup

1 tablespoon treacle

1 teaspoon ground star anise

1 teaspoon ground fennel

Grated zest of 2 oranges

1. Mix the yeast with the sugar and 1/4 pint of the warm milk in a large jug.
2. Stir and leave for 10 minutes to froth.
3. Sieve the flour, spices and salt together into a large bowl and stir in the rye flour.
4. Pour the rest of the milk and the melted butter into the yeast mixture.
5. Make a well in the centre of the flour and add the orange zest, yeast mixture, syrup and treacle.
6. Mix thoroughly with a wooden spoon till all the flour is combined with the other ingredients.
7. Knead the dough for 5-10 minutes until the mixture is smooth.
8. Cover and leave to prove in a bowl for 45 mins.
9. Knock back and knead for a further 3-4 mins.
10. Divide the dough into 3 equal parts and form into smooth round loaves.
11. Place on an oiled baking sheet, cover and prove for 30 minutes.
12. Brush with water and bake at 200ºC/Gas mark 6 for 30-35 minutes.
13. Leave to cool thoroughly before slicing.

Pumpernickel

 **DIFFICULTY**
Easy

 PREP TIME 75 mins
BAKE TIME 45-55 mins

Pumpernickel is a dark rye bread that stores well and is good served with sliced meats, cheese and pickles. We like to eat it with tomatoes seasoned with salt and vinegar. **This bread must be stored for 1-2 days before eating to allow the flavour to develop.**

INGREDIENTS

150 g/5 oz dark rye flour

700 g/1 1/2 lb. wholemeal flour

90 g/3 oz buckwheat flour

50 g/3 oz cornmeal (semolina)

2 sachets fast action dried yeast

2 teaspoons salt

1 tablespoon treacle

750 ml/1 1/4 pints warm water

1. Mix the flours and salt in a large bowl and stir in the yeast.
2. Make a well in the centre and pour in half of the water and the treacle.
3. Mix together then add the rest of the water, mixing well with a wooden spoon.
4. Knead the dough for 10-15 minutes until it becomes smooth and elastic.
5. Oil two 2 lb. loaf tins and shape the dough into two loaf shapes, place in the tins and leave to prove for 50 minutes. The dough should rise to just above the tins.
6. Bake at 190ºC/Gas mark 6 for 45-50 minutes. If the dough isn't cooked after this time, cook for a further 10 minutes, checking for burning.

Grissini

 DIFFICULTY Easy

 PREP TIME 40 mins
BAKE TIME 10-12 mins

There are many wonderful Italian bread recipes from all the different regions throughout the country. I have included the most popular eaten in Britain and my son's own favourite, Grissini.

INGREDIENTS

500 g/1 lb. plain white flour

1 sachet fast action dried yeast

3 teaspoons salt

1 tablespoon sugar

1 tablespoon olive oil

300 ml/1 pint warm water

1. Mix the flour, salt, sugar and yeast together in a bowl and add the water and oil.
2. Combine well with a wooden spoon and knead for 10 minutes.
3. Leave to prove for 30 minutes.
4. Break off small sections of dough and roll and stretch each piece until each one measures around 30 cm/12 inches long.
5. Place on an oiled baking sheet. Brush each stick with a little olive oil and sprinkle with sesame or poppy seeds if you wish.
6. Bake at 190°C/Gas mark 6 for 10 - 12 minutes.

Ciabatta

 DIFFICULTY
Easy

 PREP TIME 4.5 hours
BAKE TIME 15-20 mins

Ciabatta is one of the most popular breads in Italy and Britain alike. It needs to be left to prove for long periods of time, during which the characteristic large holes are formed in the bread, so this stage cannot be rushed. This is a recipe I have adapted to make an easy and much quicker version.

INGREDIENTS

500 g/1 lb. strong
white flour

1 sachet fast action
dried yeast

2 teaspoons salt

380 ml/14 fl oz water

1. Sieve the flour and salt together into a bowl and stir in the yeast.
2. Add the water gradually and knead in to make a smooth dough.
3. Continue to knead for a further 10 minutes and shape into two long, flat loaves.
4. Place on a lightly oiled baking tray and leave to prove for 3-4 hours in a cool place. NOT A WARM PLACE!
5. Bake for 15-20 minutes at 220ºC/Gas mark 7.

Focaccia

 DIFFICULTY
Intermediate

 PREP TIME 1 hour
BAKE TIME 25-30 mins

Focaccia has many names in different regions of Italy, from 'Schiacciata' in Tuscany to 'Fitascetta' in Lombardy. We call it Focaccia, but whatever it is called it is a flat bread made with lots of lovely olive oil and coarse sea salt. Focaccia is an ancient bread and dates back to when baking was carried out on hot stones over an open fire. After proving, the dough is pressed flat in an oiled tray and indentations are made in the dough using the fingers. These indentations are there to catch the olive oil during the baking process. This loaf was originally made popular by the Romans and has changed very little, though there are many variations cooked throughout Italy.

This loaf is traditionally cooked in an oven after the fire has been raked down, but the temperature is still too hot to cook the larger loaves without them burning. Focaccia can be eaten as an accompaniment to main dishes or soups and it makes an excellent shared starter to a meal served with olives and sun-dried tomatoes. This recipe is the simplest form, but one which can be varied quite readily.

INGREDIENTS

500 g/1 lb. 2 oz strong white flour

1 sachet fast action dried yeast

Approximately 180 ml/6 fl oz warm water

1/2 teaspoon salt

2 tablespoons olive oil plus a little extra for drizzling over the finished bread

20 g/1 oz coarse sea salt

1. Put the flour, yeast and salt in a bowl and mix.
2. Add the oil and water and mix together thoroughly.
3. Knead the dough for about 10 minutes until smooth and elastic. Leave to prove in a warm place for 40 minutes.
4. Heat the oven to 225ºC/Gas mark 7.
5. After proving press the dough out onto an oiled baking tray until it measures about 2cm in thickness. Press the fingertips into the dough to make indentations and drizzle with olive oil.
6. Sprinkle with sea salt and bake for about 25

minutes until golden brown, then drizzle more oil over the hot bread.

7. Allow to cool and cut into rectangles.

Variations on a theme

If you like it savoury
This recipe can be varied by topping the bread with onions, sliced olives or thinly sliced courgettes. Various cheeses can also be sprinkled on top to add flavour.

If you like it sweet
The Tuscan version 'Schiacciata' is a sweetened bread that has sugar, eggs and spices added.

If you like cheese
A really tasty version is Focaccia 'al formaggio' where two thin layers of dough are rolled out and stracchino cheese spread over the layers and drizzled with olive oil and baked until the cheese melts. Some regions use polenta or buckwheat flour to make the dough.

Bread Recipes From Around The World   79

French Baguette

 DIFFICULTY
Easy

 PREP TIME 1 hour
BAKE TIME 15-20 mins

The French love their fresh bread and, despite their huge supermarkets, the local traditional boulangerie still continues to provide much of the nations daily fresh bread. When we were on holiday on a little Northern French hamlet, the local baker came around selling his fresh baguettes and rolls every morning. It is difficult to achieve the same texture and taste of real French bread, but the following recipes are still delicious and reminiscent of the freshest bread you would find in France.

INGREDIENTS

450 g/1 lb. strong white flour

1 sachet fast action dried yeast

1 teaspoon salt

300 ml/ 1/2 pint warm water

Egg to glaze

1. Sieve the flour and salt together into a bowl and stir in the yeast.
2. Mix in the warm water and knead for 10 minutes. Leave to prove in a warm place for 20 minutes.
3. Knock back and knead for a few more minutes.
4. Divide into 3 equal sections and shape into a 30 cm/12 inch long roll.
5. Place on an oiled baking sheet and leave to prove for 30 minutes.
6. Brush with beaten egg to glaze.
7. Bake for 15-20 minutes at 220ºC/Gas mark 7.

Brioche

 DIFFICULTY
Easy

 PREP TIME 1 hour
BAKE TIME 10-15 mins

Brioche is my favourite breakfast roll when in France and is delicious with French preserves. They keep well for a few days in an air-tight tin and are best warmed if more than a day old. The following recipe makes 15-20 brioches.

INGREDIENTS

450 g/1 lb. strong white flour

1 sachet fast action dried yeast

2 level teaspoons salt

225 g/8 oz melted butter

90 ml/3 fl oz warm milk

4 eggs, beaten

1 tablespoon golden caster sugar

1. Sieve the flour and salt together into a bowl and stir in the yeast.
2. Add a little milk, butter and beaten eggs (leaving a little to glaze the brioche with before baking) and mix thoroughly with a wooden spoon.
3. Knead for 10 minutes until smooth and pliable.
4. Break off small amounts of dough and roll into oval shapes, placing them on an oiled baking sheet. Repeat until all the dough is used. Four larger brioches may be made if preferred.
5. Leave to prove for 30 minutes, then brush with the remaining egg.
6. Bake for 10-15 minutes for the small brioche or 15-20 minutes for the larger ones at 220ºC/ Gas mark 7.

Bread Recipes From Around The World 81

Croissants

 DIFFICULTY
A bit tricky

 PREP TIME 2-3 hours
BAKE TIME 15-20 mins

Making croissants isn't easy and is time consuming, but is well worth having a go and you will see what a real croissant should taste taste like. I have made them using two different methods of incorporating the butter. The first where I chop the butter directly into the flour, as I did at school when making them for a level Domestic Science.you have to have very cold hands for this and the layers or laminations are not well defined. The second method is where you form a slab of butter and fold the dough around it. This gives lighter crisp laminations and with patience, a light well flavoured croissant.

INGREDIENTS

500g strong white flour

1 level tsp salt

50-75g soft brown or golden caster sugar, the amount depends on how sweet you like them

1x7g sachet fast action yeast

300ml warm water

300g very cold butter

1. Sift the flour and salt together in a large mixing bowl.
2. Stir in the sugar and the yeast.
3. Make a well in the flour and add the water, mix together to form a dough.
4. Roll into a ball and chill for 20 minutes.
5. Place butter between two pieces of baking paper, measuring about 40cm by 18cm and bash down with a rolling pin to flatten and almost fit the paper. Put the butter back in the fridge for 20 mins.
6. Dust a work surface with flour. Roll out to form a rectangle about 58-60cm by 20-22cm and about 1cm thick.
7. Place the butter on the bottom two thirds of the rolled out dough.
8. Bring the top unbuttered third down to half way down the butter, leaving a third uncovered.
9. Fold the top half down over the uncovered section and gently pinch the edges together.

You will have two layers of butter in between dough.

10. Place in a food bag and chill for 40 mins.
11. Take out of the fridge and have a folded edge next to you, roll out to form a rectangle as before. Fold down the top third over the middle third and bring the bottom third up over. Place back in the bag refridgerate for 40 mins.
12. Repeat this 3 more times. Leave to rest for at least 4 hours in the food bag in the fridge. They can be left overnight.
13. Grease and line two baking sheets with baking paper.
14. Roll the chilled dough out to measure 40-42cm by 22-24cm and cut lengthways to form two long rectangles.
15. Cut each strip into three squares and cut each into two triangles. You will have 12 triangles.
16. Have the widest edge of each triangle closest to you when rolling and gently roll up to the point at the top. Form into a crescent shape and place on the prepared baking sheet.
17. Cover with a clean tea towel and leave in a cooling place but not the fridge for about an hour to an hour and half. The croissants should have almost doubled in size.
18. Preheat the oven to 200C/ gas 6/400F and bake for about 15 minutes.
19. Eat warm. Any left over may be reheated the next day, store in an airtight container and eat within 48 hours.

Chapter Six

Sweetened Breads

When I first began cooking with yeast I slipped into the common assumption that it is only used for making loaves and rolls. There are, however, so many wonderful recipes for both bread and bread related products that I would never be able to fit them into this book. This section focusses on sweetened doughs that make delicious tea-breads and desserts. They are easy to make and come in all shapes and sizes. Most recipes keep better than other unsweetened doughs as they contain more fat and, of course, sugar, both of which act as a preservative. The first section covers individual buns or teacakes.

Helpful hint If you have problems with your Muscovado sugar being lumpy as I sometimes do, place it in a bowl covered with a damp tea cloth for an hour and the sugar will regain its correct texture. This happens because the sugar dries up in the packet and needs a little re-moistening.

Twin Rose Teacakes

 DIFFICULTY Easy

 PREP TIME 45-50 mins
BAKE TIME 8-15 mins

Teacakes originate from both Yorkshire and Lancashire - hence the name. They have always been a popular tea break treat. I remember coming home from school on a wintery day to a mug of cocoa and a hot toasted teacake.

Teacakes are thought to be descendants of a medieval 'hand-bread' or 'manchet'. These were small, hand shaped loaves made with the finest flour of the time and cooked without a tin. They can be made without dried fruit for those who dislike it , but personally I love the fruited version. Spices such as cinnamon and nutmeg may be included in the recipe, but I prefer to save this for hot cross buns.

INGREDIENTS

450 g/1 lb. strong white flour

1 sachet fast action dried yeast

300 ml warm milk

50 g/2 oz currants (rinsed and dried)

50 g/2 oz sultanas (rinsed and dried)

40 g/1.5 oz softened butter

50 g/2 oz sugar

1 level teaspoon salt

1. Mix the flour and salt together in a large mixing bowl and add the yeast.
2. Rub in the butter and add the sugar.
3. Make a well in the centre of the flour and add the milk, stirring well. Knead the dough until smooth.
4. Next, knead in the dried fruit and continue to knead for a further 5 minutes.
5. Divide the dough into 10-12 small balls, knead into ball shapes and roll into 9 cm discs.
6. Place on an oiled baking tray and leave to prove for 20-30 minutes.
7. Bake in a hot oven at 225°C/Gas mark 8 for 10 minutes.
8. Cool and serve with butter and/or some homemade preserve or honey.

Sweetened Breads   85

Farthing Buns

 DIFFICULTY
Easy

 PREP TIME 45 mins
BAKE TIME 10-12 mins

In the later years of Queen Victoria's reign Farthing buns, as the name suggests, cost a farthing each, which was quite expensive at the time. They are very rich and buttery and a real treat. This recipe makes between 20 and 25 buns.

INGREDIENTS

450 g/1 lb. strong white flour

1 sachet fast action dried yeast

220 ml/8 fl oz warm milk or milk and water mixed

1/2 teaspoon salt

100 g/4 oz unrefined caster sugar

50 g/2 oz butter, gently melted but not hot

125 g/4 oz mixed dried fruit

1 large egg, beaten

Unrefined granulated sugar for sprinkling and melted butter for brushing

1. Sieve the flour and salt together and stir in the yeast and sugar.
2. Add the liquid, butter and beaten egg (saving a little to glaze the buns with). Mix thoroughly with a wooden spoon.
3. Add the dried fruit gradually whilst kneading it in with your hands. Keep kneading the dough for 8 minutes, then leave to prove for 20 minutes.
4. Roll out the dough to a rectangle about 5 mm/ 1/4 inch thick and brush with melted butter over the top two thirds of the dough.
5. Fold the unbuttered third up over the centre section and the remaining section over the others. Leave the rest for 10 minutes.
6. Roll out the dough in the same way, but brush the whole surface with butter and sprinkle with sugar.
7. Then cut the dough into rectangles approx. 8 cm/3 inches by 3 cm/11/4 inches and place them on an oiled baking sheet. Leave to prove in a warm place for 20-30 minutes.
8. Bake for 10-12 minutes at 220ºC/Gas mark 7.

Chelsea Buns

 DIFFICULTY
Easy

 PREP TIME 1 hour 45 mins
BAKE TIME 20-25 mins

My first encounter with making Chelsea buns was in an O-Level cookery lesson, taught by a student teacher. Confident about making bread I thought this lesson would be enjoyable but, during the process of rolling out the dough and sprinkling the work surface with what I thought was flour in a shaker, my dough began running off the table like a grey, yeasty liquid. The poor student teacher was flabbergasted, but my usual teacher had an explanation: 'There is icing sugar in your shaker, not flour. You have over-fed your yeast, Diana. You will have to start again.' I did and they turned out fine.

INGREDIENTS

250 g/8 oz strong white flour

1 teaspoon dried yeast

1/2 teaspoon sugar, for the yeast

90 ml/1 oz warm milk

25 g/1 oz melted butter

1/2 teaspoon salt

1 egg, beaten

75 g/3 oz raisins

1 tablespoon candied peel

25 g/1 oz melted butted for brushing over the dough

50 g/2 oz demerara sugar

Honey for glazing

1. Mix the dried yeast with the sugar and warm milk and leave to froth up for 10 minutes.
2. Meanwhile, sieve the flour and salt into a bowl and add the yeast mixture, butter and beaten egg.
3. Mix together and knead until smooth for about 10 minutes. Cover the dough and leave in a warm place to prove for about 40 minutes.
4. Roll out the dough into a rectangle measuring about 32 cm by 22 cm/13 inches by 9 inches.
5. Brush with melted butter and sprinkle with sugar, dried fruit and peel.
6. Starting with the longest edge, roll up the dough into a long sausage shape and cut out 9 slices.
7. Place each slice cut side up on an oiled baking sheet. Keep them close together as they should meet when they are cooking.
8. Leave to prove for 30 minutes and then bake for 20-25 minutes at 220°C/Gas mark 7 till golden brown.
9. Brush the hot buns with honey to glaze.

Sweetened Breads

Bath Buns

 DIFFICULTY
Easy

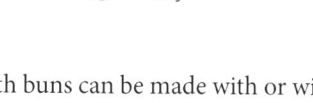 PREP TIME 50 mins
BAKE TIME 10-12 mins

Bath buns can be made with or without fruit, depending on your preference. If you want to omit the fruit from the following recipe just exclude it, but do add the grated lemon zest as this lifts the flavour of the buns. They are very easy to make and this will provide about 15 buns.

INGREDIENTS

275 g/10 oz strong white flour

25 g/1 oz unrefined caster sugar

150 ml/ 1/4 pint warm milk

75 g/3 oz melted butter

1/2 sachet fast action dried yeast

1 egg. beaten

Zest of 1 lemon

100 g/4 oz sultanas

25 g/1 oz candied peel

50 g/2 oz crushed brown lump sugar or sugar cubes

1. Sieve the flour and salt into a bowl and stir in the sugar and yeast.
2. Pour in the warm milk, butter and egg. Mix together well with a wooden spoon.
3. Knead in the fruit, peel, lemon zest and crushed sugar and continue to knead for 10 minutes.
4. Divide the dough into 15 equal pieces, place on an oiled baking tray and leave to prove for 30-35 minutes.
5. Brush with milk and sprinkle each bun with a little more crushed sugar.
6. Bake for 10 minutes at 220ºC/Gas mark 7.

Honey and Raisin Buns

 DIFFICULTY
Easy

 PREP TIME 15 mins
BAKE TIME 15-20 mins

These soft buns owe their light texture to their yoghurt and egg white content. They don't contain yeast so are very quick to make. This recipe makes about 12 buns.

INGREDIENTS

---

300 g/10 oz plain flour

2 teaspoons baking powder

1/2 teaspoon salt

50 g raisins

2 tablespoons honey

300 ml/10 fl oz plain runny yoghurt

2 whisked egg whites

1. Sieve the flour, salt and baking powder together into a bowl.
2. Stir in the yoghurt, honey and raisins and fold in the egg whites.
3. Put a heaped tablespoon of the mixture into each compartment of a non-stick muffin tin and bake for 15-20 minutes at 220ºC/Gas mark 7.

Sweetened Breads   89

Lemon Curd Buns

 DIFFICULTY
Easy

 PREP TIME 40 mins
BAKE TIME 10-12 mins

When I serve these buns to friends and family I don't tell them about the hidden centre which makes for a delicious surprise. These lemon curd buns bring a smile to everyone who eats them.

INGREDIENTS

400 g/14 oz strong white flour

1 sachet fast action dried yeast

1/2 level teaspoon salt

75 g/3 oz sugar

1 egg, beaten

220 ml/8 oz warm water

75 g/2 oz melted butter

Lemon curd for filling

Melted butter for brushing the dough

Beaten egg to glaze

Unrefined caster sugar to sprinkle on buns

1. Sieve most of the flour and salt together and stir in the sugar and yeast.
2. Pour in the water and butter and mix thoroughly.
3. Add the beaten egg and the rest of the flour and knead well for 10 minutes to make a smooth dough. Leave to prove for 20 minutes.
4. Break off small amounts of dough and roll them into small discs, about 3 mm thick.
5. Brush with butter and place a teaspoon of lemon curd in the centre of the disc. Fold in half and seal the edges well.
6. Brush once more with butter and fold and seal again. Place on an oiled baking sheet and leave to prove for 20 minutes.
7. Brush with beaten egg and sprinkle with sugar.
8. Bake for 10-12 minutes at 220ºC/Gas mark 7.

Sally Lunn Loaf

 **DIFFICULTY**
Easy

 PREP TIME 45 mins
BAKE TIME 15-20 mins

The next recipe can be made into 3 medium sized loaves as described or individual rolls. This recipe will make about 8 individual rolls. The Sally Lunn loaf is named after the lady who first made it. Sally Lunn was a celebrated pastry cook who lived in Bath in the 1780's and owned a shop in Lilliput Alley. She sold her wares to the rich and fashionable people of the time who came to sample the local waters. The cakes and breads were sold in the Pump Room and eaten alongside the drinking of the water. Her shop is still there to visit.

This loaf is best eaten warm with generous amounts of butter, but be careful when slicing. Use a very sharp knife as it can be tricky.

INGREDIENTS

280 g/10 oz. strong white flour

1 sachet fast action dried yeast

150 ml/5 fl oz warm water

40 g/1 1/2 oz sugar

50 g/2 oz softened butter

1 large egg, beaten

Finely grated rind of 1 lemon

1/2 teaspoon salt

1. Sift the flour into a bowl and stir in the salt.
2. Add the yeast and mix thoroughly.
3. Make a well in the centre of the flour and add the sugar, egg and lemon rind. Add the water and mix in vigorously.
4. Next, knead in the butter and continue to knead the dough till smooth for approximately 5 minutes.
5. Divide the dough into 3 equal parts and knead each section, shaping each one into a round and place them on an oiled baking tray, leaving them to prove in a warm place for about 30 minutes.
6. Brush with beaten egg and bake in a hot oven at 225°C/Gas mark 8 for 15 minutes.

Sweetened Breads

Selkirk Bannocks

 DIFFICULTY
Easy

 PREP TIME 1 hour
BAKE TIME 20 mins

The bannock is a flat loaf the size of a large tea plate. It is this shape because it was traditionally cooked on a flat griddle pan. They contain a lot of fruit so they are very wholesome. This recipe makes 3 good sized loaves.

INGREDIENTS

450 g/1 lb. strong
white flour

1 sachet fast action
dried yeast

1 level teaspoon salt

60 g/2 oz sugar

80 g/3 oz melted butter

450 g/1 lb. sultanas or
a mixture of raisins,
currants and sultanas

300 ml/ 1/2 pint
warm milk

Honey to glaze

1. Sieve the flour and salt together into a bowl and stir in the yeast and sugar.
2. Make a well in the centre and add the milk and butter. Mix thoroughly until all the ingredients are combined and knead in the fruit and continue to knead for a further 10 minutes.
3. Shape the dough into 3 rounds and flatten well with the hands.
4. Place on an oiled baking sheet and leave to prove for 30-40 minutes. Flatten the bannocks a little with your hands again if they have puffed up too much.
5. Bake for 20 minutes at 220ºC/Gas mark 7.

Marmalade Tea Loaf

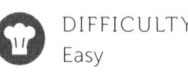 DIFFICULTY
Easy

 PREP TIME 15 mins
BAKE TIME 55-65 mins

Tea loaves are wonderfully versatile and just the thing to serve with hot drinks when people visit or even when you are peckish. Some recipes produce a bread like finish because they contain yeast, whereas others are more like cake in texture as the raising agent used is baking powder. This means that there is a great variety of tea loaf recipes, many of them very easy to make.

For this recipe, the marmalade gives the loaf a really tangy flavour and it has the added benefit of keeping it moist, which some tea loaves lack. Just because we are going to drink tea with them, it doesn't mean they should be dry. The other benefit of this recipe is that you don't need butter and is delicious eaten without.

INGREDIENTS

200 g/8 oz self raising flour

1 teaspoon cinnamon

100 g/4 oz butter, cut into small pieces

60 g/2 1/2 oz Muscovado sugar

1 egg

3 tablespoons marmalade

3 tablespoons milk

A little extra marmalade for the top

1. Sift the flour and cinnamon into a bowl. Add the butter and rub in with the fingertips.
2. When the mixture looks like breadcrumbs stir in the sugar.
3. Beat the egg and mix the milk and marmalade together. Add the milk mixture and the beaten egg. Beat these in with a wooden spoon.
4. Transfer the mixture to a greased 1 lb. loaf tin and cook for 55-65 minutes in a pre-heated oven at 160ºC/gas mark 3.
5. When the cooking time is complete, cool slightly and brush the top of the cake with a little warmed marmalade. This can be done by using a hot spoon to hold the marmalade whilst brushing the top of the loaf.

Pecan Tea Loaf

 DIFFICULTY
Easy

 PREP TIME 55 mins
BAKE TIME 15-20 mins

This recipe is for Pecan bread but you can use walnuts or whichever nut you prefer. It is also very easy if you use the fast action dried yeast and is very similar to making bread. The dough must be kneaded and, as it contains dried fruit and nuts, some people prefer to add these whilst they knead the dough, but I find it easier to put the fruit and nuts in the mixture before adding the liquid. Either way the finished loaf is the same.

INGREDIENTS

450 g/1 lb. strong white flour

1 teaspoon salt

1 sachet fast action dried yeast

40 g/1 1/2 oz unrefined caster sugar

50 g/2 oz butter

280 ml/10 fl oz milk

50 g/2 oz pecans

220 g/9 oz dried fruit (a mixture of sultanas, raisins and chopped apricots or your favourite mixture)

1. Put the butter and milk in a pan over a very low heat till the butter has melted. Meanwhile, sieve the flour and salt into a large mixing bowl.
2. Add the dried yeast and stir.
3. Mix in the sugar and dried fruit and nuts.
4. Make a well in the centre of the flour mixture and pour in the butter and milk.
5. Stir thoroughly with a wooden spoon and then knead the dough for 10 minutes.
6. Place in a greased tin and leave to prove in a warm place for 35-40 minutes.
7. Bake at 225ºC/gas mark 7 for 15-20 minutes.

Bara Brith

 DIFFICULTY
Easy

 PREP TIME 10 mins + overnight
BAKE TIME 90-100 mins

I have found and tried many recipes for Bara Brith, the Welsh fruited tea loaf (the name means 'speckled bread'). Some contain yeast and others use self-raising flour. If yeast is used, the Bara Brith will be more like bread and without yeast the finished product is more like eating cake. Have a go at both and see which you prefer.

The first recipe is very easy and makes for a really fruity finish to the loaf. The second is a little more work and uses less fruit.

INGREDIENTS

400 g/1 lb. self-raising flour

350 g/10 oz mixed raisins, currants and sultanas. You can also add candied peel if you wish

275 ml/ 1/2 pint of cold tea

2 tablespoons honey

1 egg, beaten

80 g/3 oz soft brown sugar

1 teaspoon mixed spice

1. Soak the fruit in the tea overnight.
2. Sift the flour and spice into a large mixing bowl and stir in the sugar.
3. Add the fruit and tea mixture, the egg and honey and stir thoroughly.
4. Pour the mixture into a buttered 2 lb. loaf tin and cook for 1 1/2 - 1 3/4 hours at 170ºC/Gas mark 3.

Bara Brith No. 2

 DIFFICULTY
Intermediate

 **PREP TIME** 1 hour
BAKE TIME 35-40 mins

INGREDIENTS

300 g/11 oz strong white flour

220 g/8 oz mixed dried fruit

25 g/1 oz melted butter

1 egg, beaten

170 ml/6 fl oz warm water

30 g/1 1/2 oz unrefined caster sugar

1 sachet fast action dried yeast

1 level teaspoon salt

1/2 level teaspoon mixed spice

1. Sift the flour, spice and salt together into a large mixing bowl. Stir in the yeast and sugar.
2. Make a well in the flour and add the water, melted butter and beaten egg, stirring thoroughly.
3. Knead the dough for 10 minutes, adding a little more flour if it gets too sticky.
4. Place the dough in a 2 lb. loaf tin and leave it to prove for 30-40 minutes.
5. After proving, bake for 10 minutes at 200ºC/ Gas mark 6, then turn the oven down to 180ºC/gas mark 4 and cook for a further 30 minutes.
6. When cooked, brush the top of the loaf with some clear honey.

Millie's Easy All Bran Loaf

 DIFFICULTY
Easy

 PREP TIME 10 mins + overnight
BAKE TIME 60-75 mins

My mum said that you only need to remember two things with regard to her famous All Bran Loaf. One is to soak the fruit and All Bran the night before and the other is that all the ingredients (except the milk) are the same amounts, i.e. one cup of each ingredient. How easy is that?

INGREDIENTS

1 cup (250ml) All Bran

1 cup (250ml) sultanas and raisins

1 cup (250ml) tea

1 cup (250ml) unrefined sugar

1 cup (250ml) self-raising flour

5 tablespoons milk

1. Mix the All Bran, fruit and tea and leave overnight.
2. Stir in the flour, milk and sugar and combine well.
3. Pour into a buttered 1 lb. loaf tin and cook for 1 hour at 180°C/Gas mark 4. If it looks as though the top of the loaf is cooking too quickly, turn the heat down to 170°C/Gas mark 4 and cover the top with foil.

Helpful hint Sometimes, for a change, Mum would make it with chopped dates and walnuts in place of the dried fruit stated in this recipe. So long as it is just 1 cup you could use any dried fruits or a combination of fruit and nuts. They were all delicious sliced with a good slathering of butter. Leave to mature for 24 hours before eating if you can. My mum had to hide it from us until it was ready to eat.

Sweetened Breads

Farmhouse Malt Loaf

 DIFFICULTY
Easy

 PREP TIME 10-15 mins
BAKE TIME 60-75 mins

This recipe is for a true malt loaf. It is good served with a strong flavoured cheese like Stilton or farmhouse cheddar. This malt loaf must also be left for 2-3 days to allow the flavours to develop and for it to moisten and acquire that traditional sticky texture. It is also easy to overbake it as the colour is dark to begin with and it takes quite a long time to cook. Always check the loaf after about 50 minutes by testing how firm the mixture is. If it has stopped being too springy then it is probably cooked. It will depend on your oven and, as with all the recipes, you know your own oven. The temperatures and cooking times are only a guide.

INGREDIENTS

225 g/ 1/2 lb. self-raising flour

225 g/ 1/2 lb. sultanas

50 g/2 oz Muscovado sugar

170 g/6 fl oz malt extract

1 tablespoon black treacle

2 eggs

150 ml/5 fl oz tea

1. Sift the flour into a bowl and stir in the fruit.
2. Heat the malt, treacle and sugar gently in a pan, then pour over the flour and stir.
3. Add the beaten eggs and tea.
4. Beat the mixture well until smooth and completely combined.
5. Pour into 2 buttered 1lb. loaf tins and bake for 1 hour at 150ºC/gas mark 2.

Helpful hint ▶ If you have difficulty finding malt extract, try your local health food store or home brew shop as they usually sell it. It also comes in handy when you are making your own beer. Do remember that malt for cooking attracts no VAT but for brewing purposes it does. How confusing!

Apple Bread

 DIFFICULTY
Easy

 PREP TIME 65 mins
BAKE TIME 25-35 mins

This delicious treat makes a wonderful after-lunch dessert instead of a cake.

INGREDIENTS

For the dough

1 kg/2 lb. 2 oz strong white flour

2 sachets fast action dried yeast

250 ml/8 fl oz warmed milk

220 g/8 oz unrefined caster sugar

1 teaspoon salt

200 g/6 oz melted butter

3 eggs

For the topping

2 sliced dessert apples or 1 large Bramley

2 tablespoons Demerara sugar

1 level teaspoon cinnamon

A little grated nutmeg

Melted butter for brushing

1. For the dough, sieve the flour and salt together and stir in the sugar and yeast.
2. Make a well in the centre of the flour and pour in the milk, eggs and melted butter.
3. Stir all the ingredients together and combine and knead the dough by hand for 8-10 minutes until smooth. Leave to prove for 20 minutes.
4. Oil a 30 cm by 20 cm non-stick roasting tin. Roll out the dough to fit the tin.
5. Brush the dough with butter and place the apple slices in neat rows up and down the dough, overlapping them. Leave to prove for 15 minutes.
6. Sprinkle the sugar and spices over the top and bake at 200ºC/Gas mark 6 for 25-35 minutes until golden brown.

Sweetened Breads 99

Chocolate Bread

 DIFFICULTY
Intermediate

 PREP TIME 55 mins
BAKE TIME 25-30 mins

For those who love chocolate, try this chocolate bread. I was sceptical at first about this one but once I had tasted it I was hooked. The smell when cooking is amazing and even had my neighbour knocking on the door asking me what I was baking.

This is tricky as you cannot tell when it is cooked as it is already brown, so touch the surface of the crust. It should feel firm. Also, take it out of the tin using an oven glove and test the base for the thudding sound which indicates a fully cooked loaf. See the 'techniques' chapter for a full description of this process.

INGREDIENTS

350 g/12 oz strong white flour

3 tablespoons cocoa powder

50 g/2 oz soft brown sugar

1 sachet fast action dried yeast

1 teaspoon salt

30 g/1 1/2 oz melted butter

250 ml/9 fl oz warm milk

100 g/40 oz dark chocolate, broken into pieces

1. Sieve the flour, cocoa and salt into a bowl and stir in the sugar and yeast.
2. Add the milk and melted butter and mix together well. Knead for 10 minutes.
3. Flatten the dough, press in some of the chocolate and knead again for a few seconds. Repeat this until all the chocolate has been incorporated.
4. Place in an oiled 1 lb. loaf tin and leave to prove for 30-40 minutes.
5. Bake at 220ºC/Gas mark 7 for 20-30 minutes.

Doughnuts

 **DIFFICULTY**
Easy

 PREP TIME 35 mins
BAKE TIME 5-7 mins/doughnut

Doughnuts are very popular and, so long as you have a good deep fat frying pan, they are quite easy to make. Plain white flour can be used in this recipe as it gives the doughnuts a more cake like texture.

INGREDIENTS

400 g/1 lb. plain white flour

1 sachet fast action dried yeast

100 g/3 1/2 oz caster sugar

1 egg, beaten

50 g/2 oz melted butter

1 level teaspoon salt

230 ml/8 fl oz warm milk

Sugar for sprinkling over the doughnuts

1. Sieve the flour and salt together into a bowl and stir in the sugar and yeast.
2. Add the milk, egg and butter and stir well.
3. Use your hands to combine and form a soft dough.
4. Knead for about 5 minutes until the dough is smooth and not sticky. I don't bother making rings. I simply roll out the dough into small balls. It is easier when proving and they taste equally as good.
5. Leave the dough balls to prove for 20 minutes on a lightly oiled baking sheet.
6. Meanwhile, heat your frying pan or deep fat fryer until very hot and fry a small piece of dough to test the heat. It should begin frying immediately, otherwise your doughnuts will be very greasy and inedible.
7. Fry the doughnuts in batches of 4-5, taking great care to drain the oil away and placing them on kitchen paper before finally rolling them in sugar. Frying takes 5-7 minutes depending on the size of the doughnut.

Sweetened Breads

Fruit Savarin

DIFFICULTY
Easy

PREP TIME 55 mins
BAKE TIME 25-30 mins

A savarin is very similar to a rum baba but is larger and is often laden with fruit. They make an excellent dessert and are an unusual finale to a dinner party served with any kind of cream or ice cream. They are traditionally laced with rum, but this is optional. Brandy or fruit liqueurs or simply fruit juices are an alternative. You will need a savarin or a ring mould to cook the dessert in.

INGREDIENTS

For the dough

180 g/6 oz strong white flour

1/2 sachet fast action dried yeast

1/2 level teaspoon salt

2 tablespoons caster sugar

50 ml/3 fl oz warm milk

2 eggs, beaten

50 g/2 oz melted butter

For the dough:
1. Sieve the flour and salt into a bowl and stir in the yeast and sugar.
2. Add the eggs, milk and butter and mix vigorously. You don't knead with you hands for this recipe but you must beat the mixture for a few minutes until the dough becomes elastic and smooth.
3. Place the dough in the oiled mould and leave to prove until it reaches the top of the tin.
4. Bake at 200ºC/Gas mark 6 for 25-30 minutes until golden brown.

For the syrup:
1. Put the juice/water and sugar in a pan and bring to the boil.
2. Turn down the heat and simmer gently until the sugar has dissolved.
3. Add the rum and leave to cool slightly.

Baking Bread

INGREDIENTS

For the syrup

220 g/7 oz caster sugar

Either 150 ml/5 fl oz water or fruit juice

8 tablespoons dark rum (optional)

For the fruit topping

20 black grapes, halved and seeded

20 green grapes, halved and seeded

2 kiwi fruits, peeled and sliced

1 orange, peeled and segmented

10 strawberries, hulled and halved

To finish:

1. Turn the savarin out on to a cooling rack and prick all over with a skewer.
2. Drizzle the syrup over the savarin, leaving 3-4 tablespoons for the fruit and leave to cool completely.
3. Place the savarin onto a serving plate and arrange the fruit in the centre.
4. Finish by drizzling the remaining syrup over the fruit, plus a little more rum if you wish.

Helpful hint Use any of your favourite fruit in any combination so long as it fills the centre of the savarin generously.

Chapter Seven

Celebration Breads

Special bread recipes have often been saved for special occasions and celebrations all over the world. They usually have a deeply religious meaning or are steeped in family tradition. I was always impressed as a child with the huge wheat-sheaf loaf that was the traditional centrepiece at our Harvest Festival in church. This chapter includes some of my own personal favourites that I have encountered over the years and now take great pleasure in making as gifts for both family and friends.

Northern Christmas Loaf

 DIFFICULTY
Intermediate

 PREP TIME 20 mins
BAKE TIME 40-50 mins

This recipe was one my Grandma made during the First World War in place of Christmas cake. It looks a little like a Christmas cake due to the addition of black treacle to the dough.

INGREDIENTS

---

300 g/11 oz strong white flour

1 sachet fast action dried yeast

100 ml/3 fl oz warm milk

1 level teaspoon salt

125 g/4 oz melted butted

125 g/4 oz soft brown sugar

1 tablespoon black treacle

1 egg, beaten

1 level teaspoon cinnamon

1 level teaspoon mixed spice

1 level teaspoon nutmeg

220 g/7 oz currants

125 g/4 oz sultanas

125 g/4 oz raisins

30 g/1 oz mixed candied peel

Honey for glazing

1. Sieve the flour, salt and spices together into a bowl.
2. Stir in the sugar and yeast.
3. Add the milk, egg, treacle and butter and mix well.
4. Knead the dough and add the dried fruit gradually, kneading until all the fruit is incorporated.
5. Continue to knead until the dough is smooth. If the dough looks dry, add a little warm water whilst kneading. If it is too wet, add a little extra flour.
6. Shape the dough to fit into a 2 lb. loaf tin that has been lightly oiled. Leave to prove for 30-40 minutes.
7. Bake for 40-50 minutes at 200ºC/Gas mark 6.
8. After baking, glaze the top of the loaf with lots of honey.

Celebration Breads 105

Stollen

 DIFFICULTY
Intermediate

 PREP TIME 85 mins
BAKE TIME 20-30 mins

Stollen is an Austrian bread eaten at Christmas time and is one of my favourites due to the marzipan which runs down the centre of the loaf. It is very rich, filling and delicious. This loaf keeps well as the surface of the crust is sealed with butter and sugar after cooking.

INGREDIENTS

---

380 g/12 oz strong white flour

2 tablespoons dried yeast mixed with 3 tablespoons warm milk and 1 tsp sugar

5 tablespoons caster sugar

280 g/9 oz melted butter

1/2 teaspoon salt

250 ml/8 fl oz warm milk

180 g/6 oz raisins

90 g/3 oz sultanas

90 g/3 oz candied peel

90 g/3 oz chopped glacé cherries

50 g/2 oz chopped almonds

1 level teaspoon cinnamon

A little grated nutmeg

250 g/8 oz pack of marzipan

Icing sugar for dusting

1. Pour the yeast mixture into a warm bowl and add the warm milk. Leave for 10 mins till frothy.
2. Sieve the flour, salt and spices together into a separate bowl and stir in the sugar.
3. Pour the melted butter into the fermenting mixture and stir.
4. Gradually add the spicy flour to the yeast mixture and knead to form a smooth dough. A few minutes should be sufficient. Leave to prove for 35-45 minutes.
5. Knead in the fruit and nuts.
6. Divide the mixture into 2 equal parts and roll out each section or flatten with fingers into a rough rectangle.
7. Divide the marzipan into 2 equal parts and roll it into a sausage shape to fit down the centre of the stollen dough.
8. Moisten the edges and roll the dough around the marzipan.
9. Flatten the loaf and place in on an oiled baking sheet. Leave to prove for 20-25 minutes.
10. Bake for 20-30 minutes at 200ºC/Gas mark 6.
11. Brush the baked loaves with the melted butter and dust heavily with icing sugar.

Pandolce

 DIFFICULTY
Intermediate

 PREP TIME 1 hour + overnight
BAKE TIME 45-55 mins

Pandolce, or sweet bread, is a loaf that hails from Genoa in Italy and is similar to the Panettone made in Milan. It is, however, a smaller loaf though it still takes a long time to prepare and bake.

They are normally made using two sets of dough which you then combine after the first dough has been allowed to prove for 10-12 hours. Another dough is also prepared using all the fruit and flavourings in this recipe. Then the two doughs are combined, kneaded together and then left for a further 10-12 hours to prove before baking. The bakers spend a whole day preparing this bread and it is a very special and unique taste.

INGREDIENTS

For the first dough

300 g/10 oz strong white flour

230 ml/7 fl oz warm milk

1/2 teaspoon dried yeast mixed with a teaspoon sugar and 2 tablespoons of the warm milk, left to ferment for 10 minutes till frothy

1. Sieve the flour into a bowl and add the yeast mixture and the milk.
2. Knead the dough until smooth. It should be very moist but easy to handle.
3. Leave to prove for 10-12 hours. If after 10 hours the dough is leaning, or won't hold its shape any longer, go onto the next stage. Don't leave it any longer.

INGREDIENTS

For the second dough

650 g/1 lb. 7 oz strong
white flour

200 g/7 oz unrefined
caster sugar

150 g/5 oz very
soft butter

2 tablespoons freshly
squeezed orange juice
and the zest of 1 orange

125 ml/4 fl oz Moscato or
other dessert wine

60 g/2 oz candied peel

60 g/2 oz sultanas

1 level teaspoon
fennel seeds

1. Sieve the flour into a bowl and stir in the sugar.
2. Add all the other ingredients and combine thoroughly by hand.
3. Knead well for a few minutes before combining with the first dough and knead for 5 minutes until smooth.
4. Place in an oiled 25 cm/10 inch cake tin. Use one that has sides deep enough to contain the majority of the dough as it rises.
5. Leave for at least a further 10 hours and for up to 12 hours if it needs the extra time.
6. Bake for 45-55 minutes at 200ºC/gas mark 6 until the bread is a deep golden colour.
7. Allow to cool in the tin for 20 minutes before removing and placing on a cooling rack.

Helpful hint This is best eaten within 2 days to enjoy it at its best. We like to have it with a glass of the dessert wine in the recipe. If by any chance the loaf isn't finished within 2 days, it is delicious sliced, fried in a little butter and eaten with some vanilla ice cream.

Greek Easter Loaf

 DIFFICULTY Intermediate

 PREP TIME 50 mins
BAKE TIME 25-30 mins

There are lots of special foods made specifically for Easter celebrations. This recipe is made from a plaited dough formed into a ring with two or three painted hard boiled eggs placed in the centre. It makes an excellent centrepiece for an easter Sunday table.

INGREDIENTS

1 kg/2 lb. 2 oz strong white flour

1 sachet fast action dried yeast

380 ml/13 fl oz warm milk

150 g/5 oz melted butter

Grated zest of 2 lemons

4 eggs, beaten

1 teaspoon salt

50 g/2 oz chopped almonds

Halved (or slivers of) almonds for the top decoration

1. Sieve the flour and salt together and stir in the sugar, chopped almonds and lemon zest.
2. Add the milk, eggs and butter and combine with a wooden spoon.
3. Mix all the ingredients together well by hand and knead for 10 minutes.
4. Divide the dough into three equal parts. This is important as the loaf will look odd with uneven plaits. Weigh each section if necessary.
5. Roll each section into a sausage shape that measures about 60 cm/24 inches long, plait the three sections and form into a ring. Moisten the edges if you are having trouble sticking all the ends together.
6. Place on an oiled baking sheet and place the hard boiled eggs in the centre. Leave to prove for 25-30 minutes. The dough will surround the eggs and make a 'nest'.
7. Bake for 25-30 minutes at 190ºC/Gas mark 5.
8. After cooking paint the eggs with food colouring.

Kulich

 DIFFICULTY
Intermediate

 PREP TIME 40 mins
BAKE TIME 25-30 mins

This is a Russian Easter cake made from cream cheese and dried fruit and, not surprisingly, it uses vodka to soak the saffron, but if you prefer you can use lukewarm water instead. It is a very sweet bread and you may use less sugar if it is too sweet.

INGREDIENTS

450 g/1 lb. strong white flour

1 sachet fast action dried yeast

6 tablespoons warm water

4 strands saffron, soaked in 2 tablespoons vodka or water

1/2 teaspoon salt

300 g/10 oz caster sugar

250 g/9 oz raisins

100 g/4 oz chopped almonds

60 g/2 oz candied peel

1 teaspoon vanilla extract

220 g/8 oz melted butter

Glacé icing made with 100 g/4 oz icing sugar and enough water to make a thick but spreadable iced topping

5-6 glacé cherries

1. Sieve the flour and salt together and stir in the sugar and yeast.
2. Add the water, vanilla, butter and saffron liquor and mix with a wooden spoon.
3. Knead in the nuts and fruit and continue to knead for a further 10 minutes.
4. Shape into a long, rounded loaf and place on an oiled baking sheet and leave to prove for 20-25 minutes. Due to the high sugar content the yeast will work very quickly so it doesn't need a long proving time.
5. Bake for 25-30 minutes at 200ºC/Gas mark 6 and, when cool, coat the top with the glacé icing and decorate with glacé cherries.

Casatiello

 DIFFICULTY
Intermediate

 PREP TIME 2 hour 15 mins
BAKE TIME 30-40 mins

This wonderful savoury bread is a traditional part of the Easter celebrations in Naples. It uses three different types of cheese and dried Neapolitan sausage. To give the best and most authentic flavour the recipe should contain lard instead of butter and, like the Greek easter loaf, has hard boiled eggs nestling in the centre. This recipe makes six large rolls.

INGREDIENTS

500 g/1 lb. 1oz strong white flour

1 tablespoon dried yeast mixed with 1 teaspoon sugar and 3 tablespoons warm water

200 g/7 oz melted lard

1 teaspoon salt

75 g/3 oz each of Parmesan, Pecorino and Provolone cheeses

100 g/4 oz chopped Italian sausage

Ground black pepper
6 hard boiled eggs

1. Sieve the flour and salt into a bowl and add the yeast mixture, lard and warm water.
2. Mix to form a dough and knead for 10 minutes. Leave to prove for 50-55 minutes or until the dough has doubled in size.
3. Knock back the dough and flatten with the hands into a deep rectangle and sprinkle a third of the mixed cheeses and a third of the sausage onto the dough.
4. Sprinkle with ground black pepper and the final third of cheese over the top of the others. Repeat this step twice more without the knocking back stage.
5. Divide the mixture into 6 equal sections and roll into rounds. Place on an oiled baking sheet and allow to prove for 45-50 minutes.
6. Press an egg into the centre of each roll, gently pushing it in about half way down into the dough.
7. Bake for 30-40 minutes at 200ºC/Gas mark 6. The bread will keep for 2-3 days if stored in an airtight container.

Celebration Breads   111

Hot Cross Buns

 DIFFICULTY
Intermediate

 PREP TIME 50 mins
BAKE TIME 10-15 mins

These buns are baked to remember Christ's crucifixion and have been baked on Good Friday for centuries. This recipe is easy to make and they are delicious toasted the next day. This makes about 12 buns.

INGREDIENTS

---

450 g/1 lb. strong
white flour

1 sachet fast action
dried yeast

1 level teaspoon salt

220 ml/8 fl oz warm milk

100 g/4 oz currants

50 g/2 oz sultanas

25 g/1 oz candied peel

2 teaspoons mixed spice

Zest of 1 lemon

80 g/3 oz caster sugar

80 g/3 oz melted butter

100 g/4 oz plain white
flour mixed with 4-5
teaspoons cold water to
form a dough

Honey or golden syrup
for glazing

1. Sieve the flour, spice and salt together and stir in the yeast and sugar.
2. Make a well in the centre of the flour and add the milk, butter, lemon zest and fruit and mix with a wooden spoon.
3. Knead in all the ingredients to form a smooth, elastic dough. Continue to knead for 10 mins.
4. Divide the dough into 12 equal parts, knead each one into a roll and place on an oiled baking sheet. Flatten slightly with the palm of your hand.
5. Leave to prove for 25-30 minutes.
6. Meanwhile, make a pastry type dough and roll out into a rectangle measuring about 60 cm/24 inches by 5 cm/2 inches.
7. Cut into 24 strips and, when the buns have finished proving, brush them with a little water and put 2 strips of pastry on each bun to form a cross, stretching the strip to fit the bun.
8. Bake for 10 minutes or until cooked at 220ºC/ Gas mark 7.
9. Brush each bun with syrup or honey for a shiny finish. Serve sliced with butter.

Chapter Eight

Gluten-Free Breads

So many people have asked me about baking with gluten-free ingredients. Many are not totally intolerant to gluten, but find it doesn't 'agree' with their digestive system causing bloatedness and discomfort. This is due to the wheat type used in many loaves on sale in the shops and supermarkets. In recent times the the wheat grown has been developed for commercial use and many people have found this to affect their digestive system.

However, a friend of mine has been diagnosed with Coeliac disease which is a serious and debilitating condition. She has had to totally change her diet. If you find yourself having discomfort after eating gluten rich foods, have yourself checked out by a doctor, it is always worth it.

Gluten free flour

You can purchase gluten-free blended flour from most supermarkets and shops. These are usually a combination of rice flour, potato starch, tapioca and buckwheat. These can also be bought individually. Others include teff, sorghum, quinoa, gram, chestnut, millet, maize and oat flours.

Other ingredients for successful gluten free bread making

As these flours have no gluten, the protein that gives bread texture and body, this has to be replaced if you are to achieve a loaf that is different from cake in texture. The most commonly used ones are shown overleaf.

Xantham gum

This is produced by fermenting sugars. This is bought in powder form and added to the flour at the beginning of the bread making process.

Guar gum

This is made from the guar bean. It is used in a wide range of products from canned soup to baked products and yogurt. It is a powdered substance that again is added to flour to strengthen its texture. Both of these act in very similar ways with the flour. I find the guar gum gives a softer texture to the loaf, but the xantham gum seemed to give a crustier finish. It is probably best for you to try both at first and see which you prefer.

Using baking powder and dried yeast

Ensure the products you are using are gluten-free, as some baking powders use flour to bulk it out. It is always best to check the packages before you start.

Helpful hint

Testing to see if your loaf is cooked through isn't as easy as with wheat flour. Having a food thermometer is useful as you can make sure the loaf has reached 98°C/ 210°F in the centre.

Gluten-free White Loaf

 DIFFICULTY
Intermediate

 PREP TIME 90 mins
BAKE TIME 35 - 40 mins

Use any combination of flours up to a weight of 400g. Leave enough time during your preparation for the dough to rise, about 1.25 - 1.5 hours. To make a wholemeal loaf follow the same instructions as for the white loaf, but use 200g brown rice flour and 200g brown teff flour.

INGREDIENTS

1x7g sachet fast action dried yeast

180ml warm water

100g rice flour

100g millet flour

100g tapioca flour

100g sorghum flour

OR 400g gluten free white bread flour

20g sugar

2 level tsp of either xantham or guar gum

1 rounded tsp salt

1 level tsp gluten free baking powder

3 large eggs

25ml vegetable oil or melted butter

1 tsp white wine vinegar or cider vinegar

1. Grease and line a loaf tin with baking paper.
2. Combine the yeast and the warm water in a jug.
3. Sift all the flours, sugar, gum of your choice, salt and baking powder together in a mixing bowl.
4. In a separate bowl whisk the eggs until fluffy and whisk in the oil or butter and vinegar of your choice.
5. Make a well in the centre of the dry ingredients pour in the yeast mixture. Beat together.
6. Gradually fold in the egg mixture.
7. Pour the batter into the prepared tin, cover with oiled cling film and leave in a warm place to prove. This should take about 11/4 hours and the dough should have almost doubled in size.
8. Preheat the oven to 190C/gas5.
9. Bake the loaf for 35-40 minutes, after 20 minutes turn the temperature down to 180°C/350°F/gas mark 4.
10. The crust should be deep golden and the loaf firm to the touch. Test with a thermometer to see if the centre is cooked if you are unsure.

Gluten-Free Banana Bread

 DIFFICULTY
Intermediate

 PREP TIME 20 mins
BAKE TIME 75 mins

A delicious breakfast treat, this has a slightly more cakey texture but is perfect for using up bananas that are about to turn. If you wish, add 100g dried fruit of your choice to the flours when in the mixing mixing bowl.

INGREDIENTS

3 ripe bananas

80-120g soft brown sugar, depending on how sweet you like it

200g rice flour

50g cornflour

2 tsp gluten free baking powder

Half a teaspoon salt

100g butter, melted

2 eggs

1. Preheat the oven to180C/gas 4 and grease and line a loaf tin or make 12 muffins, place 12 paper cases in a muffin tin.
2. In a bowl mash the bananas and sugar together.
3. Sift the flours, baking powder and salt into a mixing bowl.
4. Whisk the eggs in a separate bowl until light and fluffy.
5. Pour the butter into the flour and add the bananas, beat the mixture well.
6. Fold in the eggs.
7. Pour into the tin or spoon an equal amount into the muffin cases.
8. Bake the loaf for about 11/4 hours and the muffins about 20 minutes. They should be well risen and deep golden on the top. Test the loaf with a skewer, push into the centre of the loaf and if it has mixture on it bake for five more minutes and test again. The skewer will come out clean if it is cooked.
9. Remove from the tin and cool on a rack. Slice when cold for best results. If making muffins place them on a rack to cool.

Chapter Nine

Cooking with Bread

Bread can be used as an ingredient or can play an important part in many recipes from croutons to puddings. It is so versatile it can be used to coat food and give it a crispy crust or as a binding agent in both sausages and burgers.

Bread can also be used in stuffings or sauces. What would a turkey dinner be without the bread sauce? Homemade pizza bases also taste so much better than bought ones and the quickest teatime dish is still 'something on toast'. It can be used as a thickening agent and even as a substitute utensil, ideal for mopping up the gravy from a stew.

Here are a few of my favourite ways of using bread in other recipes.

Homemade Pizza Dough

 DIFFICULTY
Easy

PREP TIME 40 mins
BAKE TIME 20 - 25 mins

My children always request this when they come home for the weekend, and though it can take a bit of time, it's always worth the wait. This is sufficient to make two large pizzas.

INGREDIENTS

For the dough

500 g/1 lb. 6 oz strong white flour or a mixture of one third wholemeal and two thirds white

1 sachet fast action dried yeast

2 teaspoons salt

400 ml/13 1/2 fl oz warm water

1 tablespoon olive oil

1. Preheat the oven to its hottest setting.
2. Sieve the flour and salt together into a bowl and stir in the dried yeast.
3. Add half of the water and oil and stir well, mixing in more water to give a soft but workable dough. A greater quantity of water may be required if you are using wholemeal flour.
4. Knead the dough for 10 minutes and leave to prove for 30 minutes.
5. Divide the mixture into two and press and stretch each section to begin flattening the dough into pizza shapes.
6. Use a rolling pin to finish off the shaping and place on an oiled baking sheet.
7. Top with your favourite ingredients and bake at 220°C/gas mark 6 for 20-25 minutes.

INGREDIENTS

For the tomato pizza topping

150 ml / 1/4 pint passata

1 crushed clove garlic

2 tablespoons tomato puree

1 tablespoon olive oil

Salt and pepper to taste

Herbs to taste

1. Combine the passata with the garlic and 2 tablespoons of tomato puree.

2. Stir well and add 1 tablespoon of olive oil and season. Herbs of your choice may also be added at this stage to vary the flavour. One teaspoon of dried or two heaped teaspoons of finely chopped fresh herbs will suffice.

Variations on a theme

Pizza toppings

A mixture of mozzarella cheese and strong grated cheddar is our most popular cheese mixture. The rest of the pizza toppings are up to you, but here are some of our favourites:

A can of drained tuna, anchovies and black olives go together really well.

My personal favourite is tuna, lots of prawns and some thinly sliced red onion.

A vegetable special is finely chopped red and yellow peppers, thinly sliced courgettes cut lengthways and finely sliced spring onions with plenty of black pepper.

Chopped, smoked ham and sliced, fried mushrooms.

Pepperoni and chorizo sliced thinly with some scattered sun-dried tomatoes.

Joshua's Quick Pizza Toasties

 DIFFICULTY
Easy

PREP TIME 10 mins
GRILL TIME 30-40 secs

My son is always hungry, especially now he lifts weights for a living. These were a favourite snack of his after school, and are a tasty treat for any time of day.

INGREDIENTS

1 tablespoon tomato puree

1 crushed garlic clove or 1/2 teaspoon garlic puree

1 tablespoon olive oil

Any type of grated cheese to cover two slices of bread

2 slices of good roast ham

1. Toast two slices of bread. Meanwhile, mix the tomato puree with the garlic and oil.
2. Spread the tomato mixture over the toast and arrange the slices of ham on top. If you prefer, chop the ham first.
3. Sprinkle the cheese over the ham and toast under the grill for a few seconds until the cheese melts.

Helpful hint Replace the roast ham for sliced peppers and onions for a vegetarian option, or any other topping you like.

Variations on a theme

Something on toast

This makes a really easy tea or lunch and is much more satisfying than a sandwich. Here are some ideas for toppings for your toast:

Sliced, fried mushrooms mixed with 2 tablespoons of creme fraiche and some chopped chives.

Cooked, chopped tomatoes in a little olive oil and sprinkled with a mixture of grated cheddar and cubed Wensleydale cheese. The cheddar will melt but the Wensleydale will remain in chunks.

Fry some chopped bacon and add some beaten eggs. Then simply scramble the eggs.

Mash some sardines with a little melted butter and black pepper and spread on your toast.

A quick Welsh rarebit type topping can be made by mixing 100g/4 oz of cheddar with two tablespoons of single cream, 1/2 a teaspoon of dry mustard powder and a beaten egg. Spread on top of lightly toasted bread and then grill until golden brown.

Mash some mackerel (a small tin) with a fork, add 2 tablespoons of cream cheese and plenty of black pepper.

Eggy Bread

 **DIFFICULTY**
Easy

  PREP TIME 5 mins
COOK TIME 5 - 10 mins

Eggy bread was always something we had with bacon when we didn't have enough eggs to go around. This is a tasty version of the old favourite and serves two people.

INGREDIENTS

4 slices of white or brown bread

2 eggs

2 tablespoons of single cream

Salt & pepper

A little oil for frying

1. Beat two eggs with salt and pepper and two tablespoons of single cream.
2. Dip two slices of bread in the mixture and fry on both sides in a little oil until golden brown and crispy.
3. Serve with some bacon and/or a couple of sausages.

Helpful hint Add a little grated cheddar cheese to the mixture before frying for a cheesy version.

French Toast

 DIFFICULTY
Easy

 PREP TIME 5 mins
FRY TIME   2 - 3 mins

This is very similar to Eggy Bread, but is sweet and decadent. It's delicious served with blueberries and mascarpone cheese or a vanilla cream. This also serves two people.

INGREDIENTS

4 slices of white or brown bread

2 eggs

2 tablespoons of double cream

1/2 teaspoon of ground cinnamon

Tablespoon sugar to taste

A little oil for frying

1. Beat the eggs with the cream, cinnamon and sugar (if needed).

2. Dip two slices of bread in the mixture and fry on both sides in a little oil until golden brown and crispy.

3. Serve hot with berries of your choice.

Bren and Butter Puddings

There are many recipes for bread and butter pudding and everyone has their favourite. I have never tasted one that I didn't enjoy! Most are sweet pudding recipes but I have also made a delicious cheesy version.

The real secret to a great bread and butter pudding is to let it stand for 20-30 minutes before baking. This allows the bread to soak up all the liquid and the flavours, leaving a smoother, yet crusty, finish to the pudding. Most recipes call for at least day old bread. I have tried it with newly bought, stale and everything in between and found the finished dish to be equally good. Don't worry too much about the age of the bread, so long as it hasn't started to go green and furry!

The bread needs to be well buttered and each slice cut into four triangles. It is up to you whether you remove the crusts from the bread, but for the Marmalade recipe it is best to as it gives a smoother texture. They all serve about four people.

Cooking With Bread 125

Basic Bread and Butter Pudding

 DIFFICULTY
Easy

 PREP TIME 35 mins
BAKE TIME 30-40 mins

INGREDIENTS

4 slices white bread,
de-crusted and
well buttered

80 g/3 oz currants

3 eggs, beaten

280 ml/ 1/2 pint milk

Zest of 1 lemon

2 teaspoons
vanilla extract

50 g/2 oz unrefined
granulated sugar

Grated nutmeg

1. Cut each slice into four triangles and arrange the bread in layers, butter side up in a buttered ovenproof dish.
2. Sprinkle the currants over each layer of bread.
3. Beat the milk, vanilla and lemon zest into the eggs and stir well. Pour this mixture over the bread.
4. Add a little grated nutmeg to the top and leave to stand for 30 minutes.
5. Bake for 30-40 minutes at 190ºC/Gas mark 5 until well risen with a crusty top.

Helpful hint If you like a very crusty top to your pudding, sprinkle with a little extra sugar before the nutmeg.

Savoury Bread and Butter Pudding

 DIFFICULTY
Easy

 PREP TIME 30 mins
BAKE TIME 30-40 mins

INGREDIENTS

4 slices wholemeal bread, well buttered

3 eggs, beaten

175 g/6 oz strong flavoured cheese, grated

1 teaspoon dry mustard powder

225 ml/8 fl oz milk

2 tablespoons freshly chopped chives

1/2 teaspoon salt

Lots of ground black pepper

1. Butter an ovenproof dish and place the bread and butter slices inside, overlapping them evenly.
2. Scatter the chives over the bread.
3. Mix the eggs, milk and mustard powder together and add the salt.
4. Pour over the bread and season with black pepper. Leave to stand for 20 minutes.
5. Sprinkle the cheese over the top and bake at 190ºC/gas mark 5 for 30-40 minutes or until the mixture is set.
6. Serve with a green salad or some roasted tomatoes.

Cooking With Bread

Marmalade Bread and Butter Pudding

 DIFFICULTY
Easy

 PREP TIME 30 mins
BAKE TIME 30-40 mins

This is a luxurious version of the pudding and well worth making for a special occasion. The recipe calls for Cointreau, but brandy or rum would do equally well.

INGREDIENTS

4 slices white bread, de-crusted and buttered

Seville orange marmalade for spreading

3 eggs

2 tablespoons single cream

350 ml/12 fl oz milk

50 g/2 oz raisins

1 tablespoon Cointreau

1 tablespoon brown sugar

Zest of 1 orange

A little extra sugar for sprinkling on the top

1. Spread the marmalade onto the bread slices and arrange them in layers in a well buttered ovenproof dish. Scatter the raisins over each layer, before sprinkling sugar over the bread.
2. Beat the eggs and add the milk, cream, orange zest and Cointreau. Pour the mixture over the bread and leave to stand for 20 minutes.
3. Bake for 30-40 minutes at 190ºC/Gas mark 5 until set and golden brown.
4. Serve with double cream laced with a little Cointreau.

Chocolate Bread and Butter Pudding

 DIFFICULTY
Easy

 PREP TIME 55 mins
BAKE TIME 30-35 mins

This is another deliciously different take on the old favourite. It uses brioche instead of bread, but still butter the slices as it gives a moist finish. Brioche come in all sizes so use the equivalent amount of brioche as you would bread. You may add a tablespoon of brandy to give it an extra flavour dimension.

INGREDIENTS

4 sliced brioche

3 eggs, beaten

300 ml/ 1/2 pint milk

150 ml/ 1/4 pint single cream

100 g/4 oz high cocoa content dark chocolate, broken into small pieces

1 tablespoon brown caster sugar

Extra chocolate for topping the pudding

1. Place your buttered brioche into a buttered ovenproof dish and sprinkle with the sugar.
2. Warm the milk and cream in a pan and add the chocolate when the liquid has reached body temperature. Continue to heat gently until the chocolate has melted and remove from the heat.
3. Vigorously beat in the eggs and pour over the brioche. Leave to stand for 10 minutes.
4. Bake for 30-40 minutes at 190°C/Gas mark 5 until set. Just before the cooking time is finished, grate some extra chocolate over the pudding and finish cooking.
5. Serve cold or warm with cream.

Cooking With Bread   129

Bread Pudding

DIFFICULTY
Easy

PREP TIME 35 mins
BAKE TIME 30-40 mins

This is similar to a bread and butter pudding, but the bread is broken into small pieces rather than left in slices. It combines the flavours of apple, cinnamon and dried fruit and is a very comforting dessert when served with custard. It is cut into squares and serves about 6-8 people.

INGREDIENTS

8 slices white bread

4 eggs, beaten

280 ml/ 1/2 pint milk

1 dessert apple, grated, with a squeeze of lemon juice

350 g/12 oz mixed dried fruit

3 tablespoons soft brown sugar

2 tablespoons Seville orange marmalade

1 level teaspoon ground cinnamon

1 level teaspoon mixed spice

120 g/4 oz butter

1. Break the bread into small pieces and put it in a mixing bowl. Pour over the milk and leave it for 20 minutes.
2. Mash well with a fork to smooth out the lumps of bread.
3. Add the grated apple to the bread mixture and stir in the dried fruit, sugar, marmalade, spices and eggs.
4. Melt the butter and add half to the bread mixture and beat well.
5. Pour the pudding mixture into a buttered ovenproof dish and drizzle the rest of the butter over the top.
6. Bake for 1-1 1/2 hours at 180°C/Gas mark 4. Check the pudding regularly after 1 hour. It needs to be firm and golden brown.

Apple and Blackberry Charlotte

 DIFFICULTY
Easy

 PREP TIME 30 mins
BAKE TIME 20 - 25 mins

Apple charlotte was an old school favourite of mine and then one day I was in a restaurant and ordered apple and blackberry charlotte. It was amazing! I have developed this version over the years in memory of that gorgeous dessert.

INGREDIENTS

8 thin slices white bread, de-crusted

2 medium sized Bramley apples

220 g/8 oz blackberries

50 g/2 oz butter

180 g/6 oz sugar

2 tablespoons lemon juice

Butter for frying

1 tablespoon caster sugar for sprinkling over the pudding

1. Peel, core and slice the apples and place them in a pan with the blackberries, sugar, butter and lemon juice. Simmer for approximately 10 minutes until the apples begin to 'fall'.
2. Cut each slice of bread into three equal strips and fry gently in the butter until crisp and golden.
3. Butter a deep soufflé dish and line it with the fried bread. Cover the bottom and the sides.
4. Pour in the fruit mixture and cover with the remaining bread strips.
5. Sprinkle the top with caster sugar and bake for 20-25 minutes at 190ºC/Gas mark 5. Serve with custard or cream.

Cooking With Bread   131

Summer Fruit Pudding

  DIFFICULTY
Easy

 PREP TIME 30 mins
CHILL TIME   Overnight

This is a real 'ooh, ahh' type of pudding and one of the easiest to make, yet it is an awesome looking dessert. It needs to be made the day before you wish to serve it, so it does need a bit of planning.

INGREDIENTS

---

750 g/1 1/2 lb. prepared mixed summer fruits; strawberries, raspberries, redcurrants, blackcurrants or de-stoned cherries

50 g/2 oz unrefined caster sugar

8 slices white bread, de-crusted

1. Stew the fruit in 60 ml/2 fl oz of water with the sugar.
2. Cut the bread to line a buttered pudding basin, cutting out a circle for the bottom. Make sure you overlap each piece of bread to form a seal to hold in the fruit.
3. Pour the hot fruit into the basin, being careful not to disturb the bread. Keep some of the juice to pour over the pudding just before serving.
4. The pudding needs to be full of fruit before topping it with a bread lid.
5. Allow to cool and cover it with a plate, leaving it to chill overnight in the fridge. Serve with cream.

Variations on a theme

Autumn Fruit Pudding
This is prepared in the same way as the summer fruit pudding. Use the same ingredients but substitute the summer fruits for a mixture of the following; plums, pears, apples and blackberries.

Rhubarb Breadcrumb Pudding

 DIFFICULTY
Easy

 PREP TIME 35 mins
BAKE TIME 20-25 mins

Breadcrumb puddings are similar to crumbles but use breadcrumbs instead of a crumble mixture topping. They are easy to prepare and go well with lots of different fruits. This serves 4 -6 people.

INGREDIENTS

450 g/1 lb. rhubarb, trimmed and cut into pieces

230 g/8 oz freshly made wholemeal breadcrumbs

50 g/2 oz brown sugar

25 g/1 oz unrefined caster sugar

1 level teaspoon ground ginger

2 tablespoons orange juice, either fresh or from a carton

1. Stew the rhubarb with the caster sugar for a few minutes until the rhubarb starts to soften.
2. Meanwhile combine the breadcrumbs, brown sugar and ginger in a bowl. When the rhubarb is cooked, place it in a buttered ovenproof dish.
3. Pour over the breadcrumb mixture evenly and drizzle the orange juice over the crumbs.
4. Bake for 30-40 minutes at 170ºC/Gas mark 3 until the top is golden brown.

Gooseberry Breadcrumb Pudding

 DIFFICULTY
Easy

PREP TIME 35 mins
BAKE TIME 30-40 mins

INGREDIENTS

450 g/1 lb. gooseberries, topped and tailed

80 g/3 oz Muscovado sugar

1 dessertspoon elderflower cordial mixed with 2 tablespoons water

230 g/8 oz freshly made brown breadcrumbs

50 g/2 oz brown sugar

1. Stew the gooseberries with the sugar until tender.
2. Mix the breadcrumbs with the brown sugar.
3. Pour the fruit into a buttered dish and sprinkle over the crumb mixture, drizzling crumbs with the elderflower juice as you go.
4. Bake for 30-40 minutes at 170°C/Gas mark 3 until golden brown.

 **Helpful hint**   Serve these puddings with cream or custard, either hot or cold. They even taste good the next day if covered and stored in a cool place.

Croutons

 DIFFICULTY
Easy

 PREP TIME 35 mins
BAKE TIME 30-40 mins

Croutons are great served with soups, salads or pasta dishes and making your own is very simple. You don't need to deep-fry them as they can be made in the oven. If you do deep-fry them, which is quicker, only fry them for a few seconds in very hot oil to keep them crisp but not oily. They can also be shallow fried but sometimes you just don't want another pan on the stove.

INGREDIENTS

2 slices white bread, cut into cubes

4 tablespoons olive oil

Salt to taste

1. Place the olive oil in a bowl and add the bread. Coat well in the oil and spread on a baking sheet.
2. Season with salt and place in a hot oven at 220ºC/Gas mark 7 until they are golden.
3. Drain on kitchen paper if necessary and serve.

Variations on a theme

Parmesan Croutons
These are delicious served with tomato based pasta dishes. They are made in the same way as above but sprinkle with finely grated Parmesan cheese and a little black pepper before cooking as above.

Herb Croutons
Serve these with soups and salads of all kinds. Prepare in the same way as the first recipe but sprinkle a mixture of your favourite herbs over the croutons together with a little salt before cooking as above.

Garlic Croutons
Finely chop 2 cloves of garlic, mix it with 1 teaspoon of salt and sprinkle it over the croutons, then cook as above.

Breadcrumb Coatings

 DIFFICULTY
Easy

PREP TIME 20 mins

Breadcrumbs can be used for many different kinds of food coatings for frying fish or chicken or when roasting meats. Try the following the next time you do a roast:

LAMB ### Herb & Mustard Coating

INGREDIENTS

---

200 g/7 oz breadcrumbs

1 tablespoon chopped parsley

1 teaspoon dried rosemary

2 tablespoons wholegrain mustard

1. Mix all the ingredients together in a bowl and leave to stand for 5 minutes.
2. Place the joint in a large roasting pan and press the mixture over the surface. Be generous!
3. Either stuff rolls of meat or press into an oven-proof dish and heat as necessary.
4. Season with salt and pepper to taste
5. Cook the joint as you would normally do.

BEEF ### Horseradish Coating

INGREDIENTS

---

200 g/7 oz breadcrumbs

1 teaspoon Dijon mustard

1 teaspoon white wine vinegar

2 tablespoon grated horseradish

4 tablespoon double cream

1. Mix all the ingredients together and press over a beef joint or over steaks as they are frying.
2. If using with steaks, cook the side to be coated first, then turn over and coat each steak. The quantities given will coat four average sized steaks.

PORK

Apricot and Sage Coating

INGREDIENTS

200 g/7 oz breadcrumbs

150 g/5 oz dried apricots, finely chopped

3 tablespoons soy sauce

1 dessertspoon chopped fresh sage

1 tablespoon balsamic vinegar

1. Score the skin or fat on the joint.
2. Mix all the ingredients together and press well into the meat before roasting. This goes particularly well with a belly pork joint that is cooked for a long time.

Good Old Sage and Onion Stuffing

DIFFICULTY
Easy

PREP TIME 15 mins
BAKE TIME 10-15 mins

Yes, we can buy the packet mix and quite honestly I love the most famous brand of all and do use it for speed sometimes. But there is nothing to beat a homemade sage and onion stuffing to serve with either poultry or pork.

INGREDIENTS

2 small onions or 1 large, finely chopped

100 g/4 oz fresh white breadcrumbs

2 tablespoons freshly chopped sage leaves

Salt and pepper to taste

Butter for frying

1. Fry the onion in a little butter until soft and allow to cool.
2. Add the breadcrumbs, sage leaves, salt and pepper and either place in an oven-proof dish or roll into balls.
3. Bake in the oven while your meat is cooking for 10 minutes to get a crispy crust.
4. Use to accompany your favourite roasted poultry or pork joint.

Mushroom and Thyme Stuffing

 **DIFFICULTY**
Easy

 PREP TIME 55 mins
BAKE TIME 30-35 mins

This is a delicious all-rounder, but works particularly well with beef. You can also use this with topside steaks to make beef olives, which are rolled up with the stuffing inside and stewed in a beef stock and red wine sauce.

INGREDIENTS

---

1 medium onion, finely chopped

100 g/4 oz open-cup mushrooms, finely chopped

100 g/4 oz fresh white breadcrumbs

1 tablespoon fresh or 1 teaspoon dried thyme

Salt and pepper

Butter for frying

1. Fry the onion until soft and add the mushrooms.
2. Continue cooking until most of the mushroom moisture has cooked away. Then simply add the breadcrumbs, thyme, salt and pepper.

Cooking With Bread

Lemon and Parsley Stuffing

DIFFICULTY Easy

PREP TIME 5-10 mins

A delicious stuffing for belly pork, rolled up and tied with butcher's twine before slow-roasting. The citrus mixes with the pork juices and makes a gravy that is truly out of this world.

INGREDIENTS

Juice and zest of 1 lemon

2 tablespoons chopped fresh parsley

100 g/4 oz white breadcrumbs

2 tablespoons melted butter

Salt and pepper to taste

1. Combine all the ingredients in a bowl and mix well. Season to taste.
2. Lay the piece of belly pork skin side down on a greased baking tray and cover meat with the stuffing.
3. Roll up the pork and tie with butcher's twine.
4. Roast in a pre-heated at 170°C/gas 3 for 2.5 - 3 hours.

Traditional Bread Sauce

 DIFFICULTY
Easy

 PREP TIME 40 mins

What Christmas dinner would be complete without the traditional bread sauce? This is easy to make and will become a signature recipe for years to come.

INGREDIENTS

2 shallots, finely chopped

50 g/2 oz butter

50 g/2 oz white breadcrumbs

300 ml/ 1/2 pint milk

1 tablespoon single cream

1 bay leaf

4 cloves

Salt and black pepper

1. Put the milk, cream, shallots, bay leaf, cloves, salt and black pepper into a pan and bring to the boil.
2. As soon as it boils, remove from the heat and allow the flavours to infuse the milk. This should take about half an hour.
3. Reheat the mixture and pour over the breadcrumbs, straining all the debris away as you do so.
4. Add the butter to the mixture and stir well. Serve immediately.

Chapter Ten

When Things Go Wrong

As with anything you do, there are things that can go wrong in bread making, especially if you are just starting out. I still make mistakes and sometimes have the odd disaster. Only recently I forgot to put the yeast in my mixture and was confused as to why it was taking so long to get to the correct texture during kneading. It was only when I found my yeast sachet behind the mixing bowl that I realised what I had done. I was able to incorporate it into my dough but it took some time. The finished product wasn't as good as usual and it didn't have the usual soft texture. We still ate it though!

There are many things that can go wrong in bread making. Some are minor problems which can be rectified easily, some are disastrous. This chapter will try to explain some of these problems and how they can be dealt with successfully. I always feel that wasting food is a crying shame and shouldn't happen, so read on to prevent you possibly having to throw away a batch of bread. I have also included some ideas for creatively using up any disasters.

The Mixing

The only real problem you may encounter at this stage is with the yeast. If you are using fresh yeast or ordinary dried yeast and it hasn't started frothing up after ten or fifteen minutes then the yeast is probably dead. This could be because it wasn't fresh to begin with, or because the water was too hot when making the ferment and has perhaps killed the yeast. So a fresh batch will need to be prepared with cooler water or another piece of fresher yeast, or even a new sachet.

The temperature of the liquid used in recipes calling for fast action dried yeast is also very important as the heat of the liquid will kill the yeast in the dough if it is too hot. The best way to tell is to dip your finger in the liquid. It should feel warm. If it feels hot this will kill the yeast before it has had a chance to work. The other ingredient that can affect the yeast is salt. This slows down the fermenting ability of the yeast and, if in too close contact with the yeast, will also kill it. So it is important to mix the salt into the flour thoroughly before adding the yeast or yeast mixture. This will ensure that the salt and yeast come into minimum contact during the bread making process.

The warmth of the room and your cooking utensils may also affect the speed and efficiency of the yeast. Though yeast will carry on working when the atmosphere is chilled it is slowed down greatly. This can be an advantage if you want to prove your bread slowly, but for faster results it is best to work in a warm atmosphere.

Another problem can be too little or too much liquid. The former is very easy to rectify by gradually adding a little more liquid. It is important to carry on mixing as you add the liquid because this is the time when it can easily become too much. If you do add too much though, keep mixing and begin to knead the dough. If it is too sticky, add a little more flour, but just a small handful at a time. DO NOT POUR STRAIGHT FROM THE BAG! The dough is better sticky than dry as it will be soft and light when cooked, whereas a dry dough will end up heavy and indigestible.

Always take care when adding salt. Do not guess the quantity. The recipe will be very clear as to how much salt should be added. Too much will spoil the bread as I have learnt to my cost in the past.

The Kneading

Kneading must be done properly for 10 minutes to allow the gluten in the flour time to develop and produce the soft, springy texture of bread. The soft and sticky mixture will become a spongy dough as you knead it

If this doesn't happen continue kneading a bit more vigorously. It should become smooth and springy and the stickiness should go. Add a little more flour if it is still too sticky after 5 or 6 minutes of kneading. You will know after baking bread a few times just when the consistency of the kneaded dough is correct.

The Proving

There are two main problems that can occur when bread is left to rise. The first is not leaving it for long enough and, of course, the other is leaving it too long.

Leaving it too long is easy to see as the dough loses its shape and sags over to one side or spreads and flattens down. You will be left with odd shapes that don't cook evenly. There is very little you can do to rectify this so keep an eye on the time and check the dough regularly during proving.

Not leaving it long enough isn't as much of a problem for the finished product. The bread will be slightly heavier that it should be, but overall it will still be edible.

The secret to timing the proving accurately is to keep checking it and, when the dough has doubled in size, it is ready to either bake or knock back, depending on the recipe you are using.

Knocking Back

This is only necessary in recipes which use fresh or ordinary dried yeast. By this time the dough shouldn't be sticky so don't flour your board too much for the knocking back as this can cause streaks of flour in the finished bread. A light dusting of flour is all that is required at this stage.

To ensure an even distribution of gas throughout the loaf, knock out the large pockets of gas with your fist quickly till it is smooth and give another gentle knead till the dough has regained its elasticity. The bread will now be ready to finish rising evenly without any large pockets of gas to spoil its shape.

The Shaping

Remember that as the dough rises it will lose some of its original shape, so don't waste time putting on fancy patterns or making complicated shapes. Start with a simple one that keeps its shape whilst proving. Don't be tempted to alter your breads shape during the proving process as this can spoil the finished loaf as it interferes with the gas flow through the bread and the shape will never recover.

The Second Proving

There is very little that can go wrong with this that I have not already mentioned. Just keep checking the dough and when it has doubled in size it is ready for baking.

The Baking

Knowing your oven is the key to success here. Bread needs to be cooked at a high temperature to kill the yeast (at the right time, of course) but you don't want to burn the dough. You will know where the hottest part of your oven is and this is where your bread needs to be placed at the temperature given in the recipe. Keep checking the bread after 10 minutes. Don't worry - opening the door won't make it fall like sponge cake does, so it isn't detrimental to the finished loaf. If the loaf is browning too quickly on the top, lower its position in the oven. After 10 minutes have passed the temperature may also be lowered slightly so that the bread finishes cooking but doesn't burn.

Under cooking bread is unsatisfactory as the yeast will still be able to work and the bread will be inedible. So if the bread isn't brown on the crust, leave it in the oven for a longer time. Larger loaves often look cooked but when you slice them they are under cooked in the centre. This can be remedied by lowering the temperature by a few degrees after the initial cooking time of 10-15 minutes, allowing the bread to cook evenly and ensuring the yeast has been properly killed.

If your loaf is burnt on the bottom it is either that the baking tin or tray is too thin or the bread is too low in the oven. So bake your loaf using two or three sheets of baking parchment or greaseproof paper under the loaf whilst baking. If baking in a tin, place it on a baking sheet as extra protection from the heat. If it is too low then bake the loaf in the centre of the oven to ensure an even spread of heat.

Incidentally, this is the origin of the phrase 'upper crust'. In the large stone ovens the 'peasants' got the bottom loaves which were usually burnt, whilst the gentry got the loaves from the top.

After Baking

Once your bread is cooked there is only one thing that can go wrong. It is very tempting to slice your bread as soon as you can after it is removed from the oven. However, this is not a good idea. If it is a large loaf the bread will squash down with the pressure of the knife and your hand and will never regain its shape again. If it is a small cob or roll, when you cut into it the middle section of dough will come away from the crust in a ball and lose its shape. So wait for at least 15 minutes for small rolls and 25 minutes or longer for large loaves.

Using Up Your Disasters

Have you added too much or too little salt?

Make crumbs and use them to thicken soups, curries and stews. You will not need to add as much salt to the dish if any at all, just do the taste test. Use the crumbs to coat fish or chicken. When frying again don't salt the food beforehand. These two ideas can also be used if you have forgotten to add salt as the process is simply reversed.

Has your loaf been proving too long and toppled over?

Very gently ease the dough into a bake-able shape and cook as normal. It will have lost some of its lightness but will still taste good. This is best eaten fairly soon after baking, whilst still soft. After cooling for about 30 minutes eat with soup or salads. If it is difficult to slice, simply serve it as a 'tear and share' loaf. Alternatively, cut it into thick slices as best you can and spread some chopped garlic over it along with a drizzle of extra virgin olive oil and you have a delicious garlic bread that no one will care what shape it is as long as it tastes good.

Has the bread burnt on the bottom or the top of the loaf?

The best way to deal with this is after slicing. Don't be tempted to cut the burnt bit off whole. It is much easier to get rid of the burnt areas after cutting a slice and just trimming away any unwanted crust. If it is dark brown you probably won't need to remove too much. If it's black, remove all the blackened bits, as eating carbon isn't very good for you.

Has the bread remained raw in the middle?

Sometimes a loaf can look raw and still smell yeasty in the middle, even when the rest of the loaf seems cooked. It is best not to eat this section. It may be cut away after slicing or, if it is a large a loaf, slice the whole thing in two and make a 'tartine' type sandwich. Cut away the raw bit and fill it with delicious things, replace the top and tie some string around it to secure it, then cover it with foil. Place some weights from your scales securely on top to press the loaf and leave it for an hour or so before slicing. This is delicious as part of a picnic.

Troubleshooting

Symptom	Solution
Yeasty taste	Either too much yeast or not cooked at a high enough temperature
Knobbly top during proving	Knead for longer and more evenly
Taking a long time to rise	Needs a warmer place to prove
Not crusty	Brush the dough during cooking time with a salt water solution: 1/2 teaspoon salt to 4 tablespoons warm water
Very heavy texture	Add a little more liquid next time and ensure the dough is kneaded for at least 10 minutes
Loaf has fallen to one side during proving	Rising too quickly, in too warm a place or too much yeast has been added. Support the dough and bake
Doesn't have much flavour	Not enough salt added to the mixture
Big air bubble in the centre of the loaf	Not kneaded vigorously enough.

Baking Bread

Index

A

Acids 24
Aloo Parathas 63
Apple 98, 130
Apple and Blackberry
Charlotte 130

B

Bagels 68
Baking pans and trays 26
  Baking sheet 26
  Loaf tin 26
  Muffin tin 26
  Silicone 26
Baking powder 40, 114
Bara Brith 94, 95
Blackberry 130
Blinis 72
Bread
  Apple 98
  Breadsticks 44
  Breakfast Muffins 44
  Chinese Pan 65
  Chocolate 99
  Ciabatta 76
  Coconut 67

Focaccia 77
Granary 44
Herb 44
Limpa 73
Milk 44
Mixed Seed 44
Muesli 44
Oatmeal 44
Onion 44
Pitta 64
Potato 44
Rolls 44
Rye 44
Soda 40
Tomato 44
White Loaf 40
Bread and Butter Pudding
  Basic 124
  Chocolate 128
  Marmalade 127
  Savoury 126
Breadcrumb 135
Breadcrumb Coating
  Apricot and Sage 136
  Herb & Mustard 135
  Horseradish 135
Breadcrumb Pudding

Gooseberry 133
Rhubarb 132
Bread Pudding 129
Bread Sauce 140
Brioche 80
Buckwheat 17
Buns
  Bath 86
  Chelsea 86
  Honey and Raisin 86
  Hot Cross 111
  Lemon Curd 86

C

Casatiello 110
Chapatis 61
Cheese 41
Chocolate 99
Ciabatta 76
Coconut 67
Cornbread 69
Cornflour 17
Cornmeal 17
Croissants 81
Croutons 134

D

Dough 118
Doughnuts 100

E

Eggy Bread 122
E numbers 12

F

Farthing Buns 85
Fat 21
  Butter 21

Extra Virgin Olive oil 21
Olive oil 21
Rapeseed oil 21
Sunflower oil 21
Flour 15, 17
  Brown 16
  Country Malted 16
  Granary 17, 44
  Soft Grain 16
  Strong white 42, 43, 44, 45, 60
  Wheat Flour 15
  wheatmeal 63
  White 16, 42, 43, 115
  wholemeal 61
  Wholemeal 16
Focaccia 77
French Baguette 79
French Toast 123
Fruit Savarin 101

G

Gluten-free 115
Gluten-Free 113, 116
Grains
  Barley 24
  Oats 24
  Toasted Wheat Rye 24
Gram Flour 17
Grissini 75
Gum
  Guar 114
  Xantham 114

H

Herbs
  Chives 23
  Dill 23
  Marjoram 23
  Parsley 23

Rosemary 23
Sage 23
Tarragon 23
Thyme 23

I

Injera 66

K

Kneading 142
Knocking Back 143
Kulich 109

L

Limpa Bread 73
Loaf
  Farmhouse Malt 97
  Greek Easter 108
  Millie's Easy All Bran 96
  Northern Christmas 104

M

Malt Loaf 97
Milk 45
Mixing bowl 25

N

Naan 60
Nuts
  Almond 23
  Cashew 23
  Hazelnut 23
  Peanut 23
  Pecan 23
  Walnut 23

O

Oatmeal 17

Onion 49, 65
Oven 25

P

Pandolce 106
Pecan 93
Pizza 118, 120
Plastic bowl 25
Poori 61
Potato 63
Potatoes 63
Potato Flour 18
Proving 143
  Second 144
Pumpernickel 74

R

Raising Agents 18
  Easy-blend Dried Yeast 19
  Fast-Action Easy-blend Dried
      Yeast 19
  Fresh Yeast 19
  Standard Dried Yeast 19
  Yeast 18
Rasing Agents
  Soda 20
Rice Flour 18
Rye Flour 17

S

Sally Lunn Loaf 90
Salt 20
Seeds
  Caraway 22
  Coriander 22
  Cumin 22
  Fennel 22
  Linseed 22
  Onion 22

Poppy 22
Pumpkin 22
Sesame 22
Sunflower 22
Selkirk Bannocks 91
Shaping 143
Soda 20, 40
Soda Bread 40
　Cheese Soda Bread 41
　Oaty Soda Bread 41
Soya Flour 17
Stollen 105
Stuffing
　Lemon and Parsley 139
　Mushroom and Thyme 138
　Sage and onion 137
Summer Fruit Pudding 131

T

Teacakes
　Twin Rose 84
Tea Loaf
　Marmalade 92
　Pecan 93
Tortillas 70, 71
Troubleshooting 146

U

Utensils 25

V

Vitamin C 24

Discover more with

Kitchen
Newbie

We believe the best food you'll ever eat is the food you've cooked yourself. With this in mind, we've created **Kitchen Newbie**, a place where everyone can learn how to cook great food at home, whatever your experience level or budget.

From easy-to-follow recipes to premium cookery courses, to our exclusive range of books, we're sure you'll find something to inspire you.

Visit **www.kitchennewbie.com**
now for more details

With Paul & Diana Peacock

Join Paul and Diana Peacock every day for
a brand new recipe podcast. Learn new tips,
tricks and be inspired by delicious recipe ideas
by the founders of Kitchen Newbie.

Join the fun on Spreaker, iTunes and at
www.kitchennewbie.com

22410359R00093

Printed in Great Britain
by Amazon